MW01205971

BRIDGING THE GAP SIDEWAYS

BRIDGING THE GAP SIDEWAYS

Rutherford O. Browne

The Book Guild Ltd.
Sussex, England

The Book Guild Ltd
25 High Street,
Lewes, Sussex

First published 1993
© Rutherford O. Browne 1993

Set in Baskerville

Typesetting by Raven Typesetters,
Ellesmere Port, South Wirral

Printed in Great Britain by
Antony Rowe Ltd.
Chippenham, Wiltshire.

A catalogue record for this book is available from the British Library

ISBN 0 86332 870 9

CONTENTS

	Acknowledgements	10
1	Incident of Birth (Described by Overzealous Witness)	11
2	Primary Experiment	15
3	Washing Day at the Hot Springs	19
4	Started School	28
5	Interest in Language and Difference in People	34
6	Greater Interest at School Began to Emerge	39
7	Sea Fishing	41
8	Domestic Necessities	50
9	Bonzo and Lizzy	64
10	Sugar-cane Harvesting – Sidelights	80
11	Wakes: Tamboo-bamboo: Stick Fighting	84
12	Grave Lamentation	90
13	Tales of Gupta, Kasi Kojo and Simoko – DOMESTIC	93
14	Scooter Accident	104
15	Storm at Sea	108
16	Storm in the Woods	113
17	Hunting: Kite Flying: Aberrations	117
18	Began Work in Machine Shop – Oil Company	126
19	The Corridor Incident	132
20	Transferred to Engineering Drawing Office	137
21	Special Interest in Birds	143
22	Dreams and Nightmares	149
23	Twisted Vengeance	159

24	Frolic at Rum Shop	166
25	Carnival Dance – Coronation of King and Queen	172
26	City Carnival	179
27	Odd Encounter	192
28	Village Sports	197
29	Moonlight Excursion, Twin-Sisters	207
30	Grenada Holiday	215
31	Jury Service	223
32	Twin-Sisters Revisited	228
33	Tobago Holiday	235
34	Old Village Exodus	243
35	Frustrations	255
36	Reflections	262
37	Voyage to UK, via Mexico, Portugal, Spain	272

Dedicated to the memory of George and Annaise Browne for their love and steadfast devotion to the cause of the family's education and general well-being.

Caribbean Sea

Lesser Antilles

Windward Islands

SAINT LUCIA
Castries

Mount Hillaby

SAINT
VINCENT
Kingstown

BARBADOS
Bridgetown

Grenadine Islands

La Blanquilla

GRENADA
Saint George's

Islas los Hermanos

Isla los Testigos

Tobago
Scarborough

Isla de
Margarita La Asunción

Porlamar Peninsula de Paria

Port of
Spain

TRINIDAD
AND TOBAGO

Arima

Sangra Grande

*Golfo de
Partá*

San Fernando

Trinidad

Boca de la Serpiente

*Atlantic
Ocean*

VENEZUELA

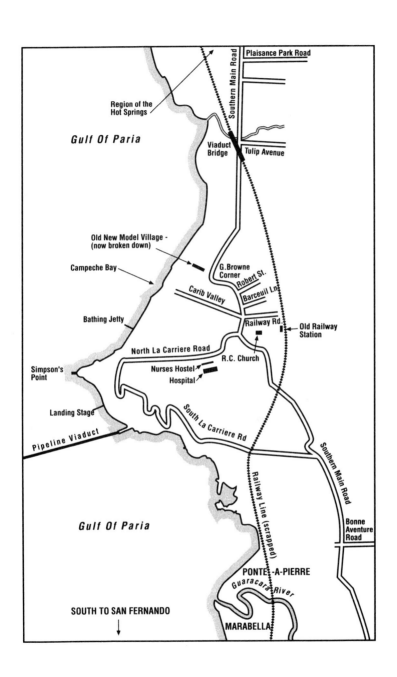

ACKNOWLEDGEMENTS

For encouragement and best wishes thanks to: Sara and Anton, and their mother, Joan Browne; Neresa Hem-Lee and Norbert Brown, brother and sister; Jacqueline Watson – artist – most helpful and skilfull operator of the wordprocessor. Jane Sherman for her sustained enthusiasm and invaluable suggestions on the matter of selected readings. Henry Da Costa Alleyne who has been of immeasurable assistance to me in every aspect of my endeavour.

1

Incident of Birth
(Described by Overzealous Witness)

From the southernmost island of an archipelago in the
Caribbean Sea, the second son of a family with roots lost
in the depths of Africa, was spirited into being. He was
born on the 28th day of April 1911. His name was Jacob.

His arrival was heralded by his own doing, a loud,
disconcerting bellow unsettled the most capable and
composed midwife the village had ever known. Auntie
Dora, as she was called by everyone, soon recovered her
composure and forthwith attended both mother and baby
with the kind assistance of Rebecca, a much admired
elder of great reputation and respectability.

'Ah, he's here! Baby's born!' Agnes exclaimed. She was
in the hall awaiting her turn to see the new baby.

'And how are you so sure it's a he?' remarked Angela.

'With a voice like that, anyone could tell it's a boy. It
don't need no brains for that,' Agnes retorted sharply with
a lingering smirk. Short, fat and moon-faced – Agnes was
a formidable character.

'Hush,' cautioned Rebecca, tall, slim and discreetly
sedate. Her smile was charming, as she raised a finger to
her lips. She had expected an imminent ruffling of feathers
between the two customary protagonists, and would have
none of it.

Auntie Dora had left them in the hall, to attend mother

11

and baby privately. But now, in response to a signal, Angela and Agnes were escorted into the bedroom to see the new-born baby. They were cautioned not to speak. As they gathered round in silence, expressions of joy and puzzlement mingled in their faces and they were quite relieved when it was over and done with.

Now back in the hall, Agnes was the first who dared to speak. 'That baby is like an old man, he. . . .'

'Hush, Agnes. Don't be so rude,' Angela interrupted angrily.

'Now look at that! You are the rude one – you didn't wait until I had finished what I had to say. You just cut across me. I was paying a compliment. . . .'

'All right, all right, what might that compliment be?' interrupted Angela, doubting the plausibility of the intended remark. The gestures of all present seemed to support that view as well.

'Well,' said Agnes, standing upright with both hands on her hips, 'I was saying that the baby is like an old man with a load of experience.'

'I must say, that was my impression too, but I didn't know you meant it like that,' observed Angela in a humble tone of voice.

An air of contentment filled the room and a high-pitched voice somewhat timidly remarked, 'I felt as though that baby knew everything about me. It gave me an uneasy feeling. I don't know what it was . . . he probably will be a man of influence, or something.'

The others murmured agreement.

Of course, I knew nothing of the circumstances surrounding the baby's birth, for indeed I was that baby – Jacob – the second son of George and Annaise, who was born and grew up in the remote village of Pointe-à-Pierre, Trinidad, West Indies, now frequently referred to as the South Caribbean.

12

Much later, at an age when I could understand such things, one of my dearest cousins present at my birth gave me a comprehensive account of the event. I saw it all as though I were there – a witness from another world.

The first moment of awareness I recalled was the whispering of a smoothing maternal voice, comforting me. It was sometime later that I remembered hearing the faint sound of a bell, which in due course I associated with the parish church. The bell was rung on special occasions, and later on I identified its clarion tones with my christening, which, by tradition, was performed at the very tender age of about three months. Long before I attained the age of adolescence, I secretly questioned the necessity of such an early baptism, when the baby was frequently rudely awakened by the splashing of cold water upon its head – an uncomfortable ritual for the hardiest of adults, let alone an infant. Despite the child's fretful protestation, the performance always proceeded in a manner which reflected an element of seasoned sadism in the whole process. And the sensitive mother could only brood as she restrained the natural desire to snatch her child away from such discomfort.

Occasionally, following such events, pent-up emotions were liberated and a somewhat jealous mother would make a teasing remark to vent her feelings.

'I say, Claudine, your little girl didn't take too well to the Christening this morning, did she?' remarked a mother after the baby in question had protested violently during the ceremony. With others looking on, Claudine could not stop herself from taking the bait and retorting briskly:

'Look here, Matilda, I always felt this was a darn fool's business and you just made a darn fool remark. You tell me woman to woman, how would you like it if someone dash a bucket of water over your head, while you sleeping?'

Claudine's unleashed fury completely disarmed Matilda, who hurriedly walked off in a huff. I was twelve when I witnessed this incident. My doubts about baptism at that tender age were confirmed there and then. The child, of course, was baptised in complete ignorance of any religious significance the ceremony may have held.

However, returning to the matter of my developing awareness, it was not until I was nearly three that an incident occurred which triggered off a fundamental understanding of my own personality. Even to this day, musing and daydreaming of the past in my distant homeland, the entire sequence of events reasserts itself with a melancholic nostalgia.

2

Primary Experiment

That particular morning the weather was changeable and periods of brilliant sunshine alternated with short bursts of rain. Remarkably young children knew the significance of these dark overhanging clouds and were always ready to dash indoors. As soon as the showers had passed, the children would continue their outdoor frolic, sometimes in the front yard, sometimes in the back, and sometimes beneath the houses on their wooden stilts.

My elder brother had just turned five. He and I were trapped indoors during a particularly heavy downpour. We knew the parched earth would soak up most of the rain, so as soon as it had ceased we dashed out into the brilliant sunlight. Our sister was only about twelve months old at the time and too young to venture outside.

I was in the habit of dashing along a winding path in our back garden, which adjoined Aunt Nenen's home. I wasted no time. Straight away I was off, avoiding the wet leaves of the fruit and vegetable plants which flanked the path on both sides. Mango, corn, banana, orange and a few shoots of sugar-cane were the main crop, although I remember vegetables such as eddoes, yam, tanya, and plenty of sweet potatoes. In the midst of all this vegetation stood a lone roucou tree, lush and magnificent. In my dash along the footpath in the back garden, I was flagged down as it were, by a large tanya leaf, bobbing and weaving to the rhythm of the rain drops, drumming upon its surface.

The effect of the rainfall had inclined the stem of the tanya plant toward the path. I noticed that the water discharged onto the foliage was channelled via a tall banana tree. I was fascinated. The surface of the leaf itself remained absolutely dry. I became totally absorbed by this strange phenomenon, by the sound of the leaf and by the way it moved. Just then the source of water suddenly dried up.

'I'd like to see more of that,' I said to myself. My curiosity was at its peak and after pondering for a moment or two, I struck upon the idea of supplying the liquid myself.

'I know what . . . let's play a game of fountain.'

I'd seen big boys doing this. The tanya leaf was just about the right height and so I supplied the water in the manner of a fountain, peeing with all my strength. However, my concentration was so taken up with my efforts to reach the right height, that I missed the effect upon the tanya leaf. With the source of my water depleted, I thought, 'Oh, I am such a little man, but one day I will grow up to be a real man.' I had always thought that the grown men standing behind bushes were engaged in watering them. My ability to provide a fountain had made me aware that I was a male. Little girls could not have done that. It was a moment of awakening.

Like most of the families in the village, we were poor. Well beyond the age of six, I was still wearing loose knee-length shirts made from old flour bags. We wore no underclothing but the material was cheap and durable, well suited to the frolicsome play of children in the yard and back garden. Moreover, the garment was ideal for dealing with urgent toilet requirements.

In those days it was usual to have large families. This

was due both to ignorance of contraception and to religious practice. The village church had a long tradition of influence upon the community.

Constructed on high ground upon a plateau, according to the legend it cast a hallowing shadow of eternal blessing over the entire surroundings. It was believed that in some mysterious way it lightened the hearts of those who were heavily laden. Several people, especially the elderly, made the sign of the cross whenever they approached its precincts.

According to further legendary tales, in ancient times all the angels of the world annually congregated upon the plateau and their soft, melodious voices were clearly heard in songs of reverence. Steeped in an atmosphere of antiquity and mysticism, the church exerted an enduring and cohesive influence upon each member of the community. Its fascinating spire could be seen for miles around and was looked upon as a landmark of great importance, not only for visitors but also for the local and neighbouring fishermen, who sighted the spire as a beacon when at sea.

As a whole, the influence of the village church in my perception, was so well established that an automatic acceptance of its righteousness prevailed in all matters.

I have no idea of any census having been taken but I imagine the total population of the village to have been in the region of 1,500, scattered over an area of approximately four square miles. This afforded ample breathing space between the houses, huts and shacks that constituted our homes.

The amount of fruit and vegetables cultivated was, in a way, a matter of each according to his or her ability. In areas where the houses were reasonably close together, it was common for footpaths to run through the back gardens, connecting one house with another. This

17

communication link served a vital purpose among the neighbours for the interchange of news, ideas and rumours of the day. Similarly, they played an important role in cases of illness or other emergencies.

The fertile land yielded bountiful crops of fruit and vegetables providing for all. The hunting of wild animals such as opossum, agouti, deer and even the occasional wild boar, provided agreeable supplements. Beef, pork, chicken and fish were also a regular feature of the diet.

Despite the fertility of the land, a high percentage of the working population went out to sea. Fishing still provided a regular occupation for a great number of men during my early childhood.

3

Washing Day at the Hot Springs

Since very early in childhood, the name 'Hot Springs' had held my attention. And, like most of the children in our remote village on the tropical island of Trinidad, I was very anxious to know what it was all about. Eventually, in her own good time, my mother responded to my repeated requests.

'Jacob,' she said abruptly on a quiet Sunday afternoon, knitting leisurely in her rocking chair in the corner of the room.

Seated at the table in the centre of the room, I was slightly startled, and replied, 'Yes, Ma.' Despite my slight apprehension, I knew my mother was not angry in any way.

'Well, it's washing day tomorrow,' she remarked with a broad, affectionate smile. 'I'd like you to come with me to the Hot Springs, how about that?' She put her question with enthusiasm and weighed my reactions.

'Oh, yes Ma, yes Ma, please. I would like to go to the Hot Springs with you tomorrow,' I replied.

Overjoyed with excitement, I made a little song of it and began dancing to the tune. My mother was still seated in her rocking chair and I raced towards her. She received me with outstretched arms and a hug which affectionately cushioned the impact.

'Well, I'm glad you're so pleased, Jacob – I knew you

would be. Mind you,' she added quickly, 'you'll have to help me.'

'Oh yes, I'll help you, Ma,' I assured her.

There and then, my mother had given me a great sense of responsibility. I felt important. I was proud. And so, the following day when all was ready, we set off to the Hot Springs, my mother balancing her bucket of clothing freely on her head and I holding my little bucket securely in my hand.

Down the hill we strode, along the Southern Main Road towards our destination, a little less than a mile away. Walking jauntily, while trying to keep abreast of my mother, I indulged her in conversation along these lines:

'Will there be plenty of people there today, Ma?'

'I don't know, Jacob. It depends on the amount of washing they have to do.'

'We don't have plenty, do we, Ma?'

'No, not so much really.'

Questions on birds, butterflies, insects and the like would most certainly have followed, as we covered the ground along our way.

By and by, a turning to the left of the main road led us to the heart of the Hot Springs. As we approached there was a general lowering of voices. Several people were already there and the momentarily muted voices showed a mark of respect for the prominent role my mother played in the affairs of the village.

After a brisk exchange of hearty greeting all round, friendly glances followed us to my mother's customary location on a partly shaded rock. As soon as we got there, a high-pitched voice rose above the others:

'We see you've brought your little boy to help you today, Mrs Browne.'

'Yes, he's wanted to see the Hot Springs for quite a

while and to help me with the washing. He's only four but he'll get some idea of what he can do for the time being.'

My mother smiled broadly with satisfaction. There was a hum of appreciation.

The lush foliage of blacksage, guava, cousinmanoe and mango trees neatly defined the peripheral boundary of our location. Much taller trees, such as the wild plum, petite feuille, bois canot, coconut and other palm-trees stood guard in the background, as though they were defenders and custodians of a sacred enclave.

In these idyllic surroundings the women busied themselves with their particular tasks. Friendly chatter and good humour prevailed, with the occasional burst of raucous laughter. A weak voice was barely heard singing softly. Someone joined in and there were two voices. Then another, then another took up the song. All the women joined together, and suddenly became a band of choristers.

The melancholic fervour with which they sang became emotionally infectious. The agonising memory of our ancestors in chains during the period of their slavery could hardly be suppressed. Then a vibrant voice suddenly broke in echoing the jubilant spirit of the current carnival. Everyone joined in filling the air with song. The transformation was magical.

The contrast of these melodies had conjured up evocative images of both the living and the dead. And, with the work yet on hand, it was most fitting to have been brought back to the realities of life. The exhilarating tempo of the calypso had quickly revitalised waning energies, and within a few moments I saw and heard the effects of the laboured lashing of garments on the rocks. A casual passer-by, ignorant of the purpose of the exercise, could not have failed to conclude that sworn vengeance was being executed for the reluctance of the garments to yield up their accumulated dirt.

However, an astonishing spectacle arose from all this. Rainbow-tinted curtains of suspended water particles dispersed from the garments during their severe battering against the rocks and hovered above it all, like a spirit arising from a watery grave. In concert with the faint lingering echoes of the pensive folk songs, they sauntered in the haunting vapour from the bubbling water of the hot springs. All around there was a profusion of flowers with an astonishing variety and richness of colour. Their exotic fragrance filled the air. Lulling butterflies calmly dodged the humming birds and the buzzing bees in pursuit of nectar.

This, my first visit to the Hot Springs with my mother on her washing day, was one of the greatest experiences of my youth. I had made several discoveries beyond my understanding and hoped to return to satisfy my curiosity at a later date. But for the moment it was to me, my Garden of Eden.

At a later stage in my development, a sudden flood of interest in the phenomena I had observed at the Hot Springs spurred me on to make some investigations.

'Ah, here is a good moment,' I said to myself and hurried toward Mr Bengie. He was a village elder and a friend to some distant relation. He was on one of his regular strolls along the beach.

'Ah ha, Mr Bengie,' I cried excitedly. 'Please, I would like you to help me with some problems, sir. If you have a minute.'

'Oh, I don't know, son . . . wait a minute now, you are Jacob, aren't you?'

'Yes, sir,' I replied, smiling in anticipation of his readiness to help.

'Yes, of course, I know you, Jacob. You growed so much I nearly didn't recognise you. Now, what is the problem, Jacob? Let's get down to the root of it.'

In those days it was quite customary for children to seek advice from any adult, often in preference to approaching their own parents and one thought nothing of it.

Now standing close to him and looking up into his white beard, I said, 'It's about the Hot Springs, Mr Bengie.'

His face lit up as though I had touched upon his favourite subject. 'Oh yes. good. What exactly do you want to know about the Hot Springs, eh?' he asked.

'Well, it's about the bubbles, really. They look so pretty as they rise up from the bottom to the surface . . . and then they disappear. Why do they do that?'

Mr Bengie hesitated. He gazed out at some distant horizon across the sea, his lips quivering a little as he mumbled to himself.

Then, pointing in the direction, he said, 'Look, let's sit down over there on that old tree trunk.'

In silence we slowly proceeded along the beach in the direction he had indicated. I knew that Mr Bengie was hard at work on the problem I had unwittingly set and I feared that he was being overtaxed.

As we approached the tree trunk Mr Bengie quickened the pace and we finally sat down. With a heavy sigh of relief, he said, 'Well now, about them bubbles we were talking about. . . .'

'Yes, sir, at the Hot Springs,' I interrupted politely.

'Yes, the bubbles in the water, of course,' he replied, still deep in thought. 'Now let's get down to the root of the matter. I like that, don't you?'

'What, Mr Bengie?'

'The root of the matter,' he emphasized. 'It's always better to start from the root of anything, my son; just like the trees and all these beautiful flowers we see about the place . . . yes, yes, start from the root of the matter. Mark my words – they will serve you well when you come to my age.'

Mr Bengie was showing signs of fatigue and I thought it unjust to put him under any more strain, so I decided to postpone my enquiry. But just then he raised a hand haltingly, as a plea for understanding.

'You know, son, I solved that problem a very long time ago, when I was a little boy, just like you. But, as the years go by, you forget these things. Life is like that, you know.'

'Yes, I understand, Mr Bengie. I was just about to ask if I could see you another time, as I have to go now,' I explained.

'Oh yes, yes, you run along now. Come back and have a chat again on any problem . . . and by the way, I agree with you. I believe the bubbles at the Hot Springs would make the place prettier if they stay at the bottom of the water, instead of coming up and then disappearing.'

Just then a loud urgent squawk commanded prompt attention. Mr Bengie's face lit up with ecstasy. His favourite seagull, Rufus, had suddenly appeared. He had swooped down onto Mr Bengie's shoulder for his customary titbits.

For several months I pondered over Mr Bengie's remark about the bubbles in the water at the Hot Springs. I kept thinking that there must be some reason why the bubbles kept rising to the surface of the water. I decided to make a close inspection and asked Alex to accompany me. Besides being much older than I, Alex was cheerful and interested in matters of general knowledge. He didn't hesitate in accepting my invitation. In due course, we set off on our exploration.

As we entered the region of the Springs, I said to Alex, 'I don't think you come here often, do you Alex?'

'What makes you say that?' he asked.

'Well, you hardly ever mention it.'

'My sisters do all the washing for the family. They don't need my help.'

'But don't you like bathing in the hot water, then?'

'No, not me. I don't like it,' Alex answered sharply and I couldn't resist sniggering.

'Too hot for you, eh?'

'Oh no, I can stand lots of heat. It's the steam going up my nose I don't like. I prefer the sea, where I can swim about wherever I like.'

Alex's remarks were becoming dismissive, so I went on to the matter in hand. 'You know, Alex, it's the bubbles I want to look at. I want to see exactly where they are coming from and follow them all the way up to the surface of the water.'

'Right. Let's find a good batch.'

It was not long before I found a good place, where a steady stream of bubbles was rising gently through the streaming water.

I called out to my friend, 'Hey! Over here, Alex, come quickly. Come and look at this. Look, there's one stuck between the rocks . . . oh, it's gone now. Did you see it? – Wait, here comes another. Up it comes, slowly past the rocks and there it is . . . Oh dear . . . See what I mean, Alex? They just vanish when they come to the top, and I want to know why.'

I couldn't hide my disappointment and Alex said smugly, 'Well Jacob, all I can tell you is that when you told me about this the other day, I went to ask someone working at the refinery and he told me that the bubbles are due to gas leaking from the centre of the earth.'

'From the centre of the earth?' I asked doubtfully.

'Yes, that's what the man said,' replied Alex.

'Well, that's not what Mr Bengie said.'

'Who? Mr Bengie, with the white bushy beard?' exclaimed Alex with disdain.

'Yes, that's right.'

'Well, Mr Bengie doesn't know anything. He just makes things up as he goes along.'

My visit to the Hot Springs with Alex ended on this rather disappointing note and we went our separate ways.

However, my regard for Mr Bengie was not altered radically. In fact, I think I admired him all the more. He was, after all, a village elder in his late seventies. Despite his long, bushy, grey beard and his slow, ambling gait, and the way he fumbled with his words and forgot what he was saying – there was something about Mr Bengie which commanded respect. I wanted to see him again and talk to him about his favourite seagull and, later, while on an errand, I altered course and took a detour to the beach. I was fortunate. Mr Bengie was seated at his usual place on the tree trunk. He was pleased to see me. The feeling was mutual and our greetings were made simultaneously. He laughed quietly as he beckoned me to sit down beside him.

'Mr Bengie,' I asked, 'how did you and the seagull become so friendly?'

'Well, Jacob, that's a long story, but I'll tell you this: there's nothing as kind as kindness itself.'

'How do you mean, Mr Bengie?' I asked, and then after a long pause, he continued.

'You see my son, it was like this – Little Rufus, though no longer little now of course, had an accident when he was a baby. I came across him trapped in the fork of a guava tree. He was frightened to death and couldn't fly because he had broken a wing and one of his legs as well. He was between the Devil and the deep blue sea – do you know what that means, sonny?'

'Yes, sir, it means that he would be in trouble whatever he did, but how did he get stuck like that?' I asked.

'It was like this. Poor little Rufus must have been pestering his mother to leave the nest and fly off with her, but he wasn't yet ready. I expect he kept on pestering her until she got fed up and allowed him to join her. He probably flew too high and got very tired. From the way

26

he was stuck, he must have dropped from the sky like a stone and fallen into the trees.'

'How could you tell that he had broken a wing and a leg?' I asked.

'Because I rescued him and put him in splints.'

'But surely, Mr Bengie, Rufus was a wild seagull and would have tried to peck at you when you put out your hand.'

'You're quite right, Jacob, quite right. At first he was bad-tempered, but in the end he calmed down. He was frightened because he was hurt and in pain. And with the noise he was making other birds would soon seek him out and attack him. Even if he wriggled out and fell to the ground, a mongoose would soon have him. Rufus knew that all right, even though he was only little then.'

'Well, I'm glad you got him better, Mr Bengie, and I'm glad he remembers you.' .

'I too am glad,' said Mr Bengie. 'He doesn't really need these titbits any more – he can feed himself now. But he comes flapping round me to show his gratitude. You know, son, some creatures act better than human kind.'

Mr Bengie had taken great delight in relating the story of Rufus. But as I left him still seated on his tree trunk, I couldn't help feeling a little sadness. Some distance away I paused and glancing back, waved goodbye. At length, he looked back in my direction and hurriedly responded. No doubt he was anticipating another visit from Rufus, his grateful friend.

4

Started School

My parents were keen advocates of a good education and, with my elder brother already attending school, my own indoctrination had been well instilled at an early age.

'Ma, Ma, I want to go to school. Ma, let me go with Leonard.' This was my frequent plea, while my brother was being dressed for school.

And this was my mother's usual response, 'All right, Jacob, that's enough. I told you your time will come . . . You're still too young to go to school.'

Some gesture of appeasement would invariably put an end to the issue, and for the moment that sufficed. Still, it was a great relief to all, when I finally joined my brother in the 500 yard trek down the road and under the railway viaduct to the old Government School. Although I was very excited, I was conscious of a strange turmoil in the pit of my stomach. I was not quite five.

'See, I am catching up with you, Leonard,' I would say as I struggled desperately to keep up with him when we were late for school.

'You can't catch up with me . . . not if I don't want you to.'

'Why not? Bet I can,' I would say.

'No you can't. I'm two years older than you, so you can't ever catch up.'

My elder brother would say this with great authority

and there was always a finality in his tone of voice, which marked the end of our discussion as we approached the school.

As soon as I started at the school, I began to appreciate the mixed community which made up our village. This was aided by the fact that many of my father's friends were Indians with whom he grew up and whose homes he frequently visited. I knew also that the owner of the village shop was of Portuguese descent, and that the overseer of the coconut plantation on the northern boundary of the village was a white man. He was only seen occasionally, proudly sitting astride his horse and always with a whip in his hand.

'Why does that white man on the horse always carry a whip? I've never seen him beat the horse with it, have you Alex?' I asked.

Because Alex was older than I, he seemed to me to sparkle with confidence, to know everything.

'Oh, that whip is not for the horse. It's to whip anyone that sets foot on the estate. He's a terrible man, you should know that,' Alex remarked.

Well, that was enough to put me on guard for life. I knew that a horse could trample a man to death if it got the chance. And I was certainly not going to give it that chance.

In my enthusiasm to learn to speak another language as fluently as my father spoke Hindustani, I began to tease my Great-aunt Nenen. She was in her seventies, very considerate and affectionate. She had long, beautifully mottled grey and black plaited hair and Nenen always spoke *patois*. She knew no other language and I soon learned to kindle her enthusiasm to speak with me.

'Nenen, you know something? Soon I'll be able to speak *patois* just like you or even better. I'm catching up with you already.'

Despite my outlandish *patois*, she knew what I meant and would reel with laughter. Nevertheless, she was always at pains to correct me in the best way she could and so added considerably to my vocabulary. In my attempt to outwit her during these teasing sessions, I used to make up an enormous number of words which I knew could not possibly exist. It was, however, a hit-or-miss affair which we enjoyed together, and from which I learned a great deal. In a short space of time I became fluent in *patois*.

More importantly, the special bond of endearment between Nenen and myself had not only been sealed, but had courted the admiration of a host of other relations, children and adult alike. The whole family benefited as a general dissemination of love and affection had been shared amongst us all.

Despite the cosmopolitan nature of our village, the only white people I ever saw were the parish priest, a small group of them who occupied a section of the church all to themselves, and, of course, the overseer of the coconut plantation. By the age of five or six, I was beginning to wonder why the white people seemed to play a far superior role to that of the black people in our district. As usual in those days, I sought the opinion of my friend Alex.

'Alex, are white people better than black people?' I asked him one Sunday in the churchyard after catechism.

He hesitated, wide-eyed, caught by surprise. He raised his eyebrows and glanced towards the heavens for inspiration. His response was emphatic.

'No, no. Of course not.' But then he thought for a moment and said, 'But they can do lots of things better than black people can.'

'Well, in that case they're better, aren't they?' I argued.

This plunged Alex into a deeper level of thought. He

was silent and so was I. After a few moments he came closer to me. There was something conspiratorial about his approach. It was unlike him to speak quietly and he rarely addressed me by name, so I knew it was a matter of some concern, when he said, 'Jacob, why did you ask if white people are better than black people?'

'You know, Alex. When there are a lot of people at the church service, lots of old people have to stand up all the way through it – old black people, I mean – and there are plenty of seats for the white people, with nobody sitting in them. That don't seem right to me, Alex. Don't you think so?'

We were both in a serious, almost sombre mood now and Alex hesitated before he replied.

'Jacob. The white people are rich and they bought all those seats, so as to keep them for themselves. But I see what you mean about the empty seats. You know something? You're quite right, it don't seem fair to me either.'

At least his explanation had satisfied my curiosity for the time being. However, it was a matter which engaged the more serious moments of attention throughout my entire childhood and, of course, into my adult life. Somehow, I now had the notion that this injustice could have only taken place with the full collaboration of the church's authority. This realisation seemed to have set off a chain reaction and gradually the web of subtle discrimination, ever-present between the white and black peoples of our village, began to be revealed to me. Had I been given the chance of a better education I would have soon discovered that such practices were inevitable, decreed upon us as a legacy to posterity by the colonial powers, in order to perpetuate their position of privilege.

In any case, from then on I disliked the idea of assisting at the altar during the service. And besides, I had likened the parson's gown to the convenient knee-length shirts we all wore as children, so designed to facilitate the urgent call of nature. At intervals during the church service the parson's gown had to be lifted up from behind by his assistant . . . very distasteful, I thought.

From time to time, such as on sports day, two or three white people would visit the school to act as judges and to distribute the prizes. My curiosity was intensified enormously the first time I saw them at school. I had never been so close before and I discreetly took advantage of this proximity to look more closely at their eyes and the colour of their skin. I admired their manners and the manner in which they spoke.

The white people lived exclusively by themselves in a select region, well away from the rest of us. There were also an appreciable number of Indians in our community, but most of them lived in their separate factions on the outskirts of the village. They were principally Hindu and Moslem. Sometimes, especially in the late hours of the night, the beating of their drums would keep me awake. Different rhythms were beaten out in different places at the same time. I wanted to know all about it. During a moment of leisure, when my father was seated on the ground in our back yard, plaiting bamboo to make fish pots, I casually remarked:

'Pa, Indians don't sleep much, do they?'

'Of course they do, they sleep as much as everybody else, but often their celebrations are held at night and extend until the early hours of the morning,' he said and then, glancing up at me, he asked with some concern, 'Do you not sleep throughout the night then?'

'Oh yes, Pa, it's only sometimes I wake up in the night. There's a type of drumming which is quite different from the rest. I can tell the difference quite easily. Sometimes there's one that seems to be calling me.'

'The drumming you hear is not all by Indians, you know, son. There is African drumming as well,' said my father. 'I'll tell you what – some time we'll all go to see some of their celebrations. You'll get a good picture of what goes on by seeing it for yourself.'

In due course our family, like others in the village, came to know all about the various rhythms and the different drums that were played, when we were invited by the Indians to their festivities.

5

Interest in Language and Difference in People

During early childhood, my interest in the colour of one's skin arose from a natural curiosity in identifying the differences between all sorts of things, whether animate or inanimate. I found the difference in shades of skin colour fascinating and I soon began to discern less obvious subtleties. I learned that the white people were descendants of French, Spanish, English, Irish, Scots and other Europeans each of whom had given their particular characteristics to the cosmopolitan nature of our community.

As my development continued, I could not understand why an entirely natural phenomenon, such as the colour of one's skin, had become responsible for this grossly unnatural white privilege. What had started as a scientific enquiry had begun to assume a disturbing moral and political significance.

My curiosity in this matter demanded satisfaction. And so after a visit to our village school down by the viaduct, by two white women and a white girl on some official business, I brought the subject up with my mother on returning home that afternoon.

'Ma, Ma, some white people visited the school today.' I told her this with such excitement that she must have thought I'd made a new discovery.

'Oh yes, who were they?'

'I don't know, Ma. I can't remember their names . . . two women and a girl. They passed very close to me, Ma.'

My mother took note of my interest and pursued the conversation. 'The girl must have been the daughter of one of the women. How old was she? Was she older than you?'

'She was only as big as me, Ma. She had white hair and blue eyes.'

'And how could you tell she had blue eyes?'

'When they were leaving they walked along the passage and the girl looked at me and I saw right into her eyes. They really were blue, Ma. I saw them.'

'Oh, I believe you, Jacob, my dear,' my mother said smiling. 'White people with fair hair often have blue eyes. They usually have fair skin as well. They are referred to as being blonde.'

Later on that evening, in the wake of the school visit, I brought up the subject of skin colour again. Both my parents took pains to enhance our education as best they could, and so there were no restrictions put on asking anything we wished to know about. I proceeded without fear of rebuke.

'Ma, how is it some people have white skin?' I asked.

'Well, they were born that way,' replied my mother. Bearing in mind our earlier conversation about the visitors at school, she added, 'And children take after their parents, you follow?'

'Yes, I think so, But what. . . ?'

'Well, look at it this way, son. Quite a long time ago it was discovered that people in hot climates had black skin to protect them from the heat of the sun. And in countries which were cooler, white people were in greater numbers. And so . . . we were all born that way. I am sure you'll learn all about it later on.'

My infantile preoccupation was partially satisfied by

this explanation, but the close-range lingering gaze of the young blue-eyed girl began to have a haunting effect upon me. I seemed unable to talk about it further with my parents; perhaps it was impossible for me to do so.

It was not much later when I remember being left alone at home for a short period one Sunday afternoon. I was thinking about the colour of skin. I was thinking about the whole of humanity. My thoughts began to run wild. I became restless and uneasy. Nobody knew. I rushed into the back garden and started talking to myself about things I could never have known. I seemed to be under some sort of spell. Fragments of far distant past lives appeared to me like dreams. I heard voices.

'My skin is not dirty,' I assured myself.

'And how do you know that?' said a voice.

'Because I always wash my hands properly before meals and bathe a lot in the sea,' I responded.

I was staring into a broken mirror in the kitchen. I watched fascinated and frightened as my distorted image faded away. I seemed to be peering through into some past generation, where the little blonde girl and I, the little black boy, were playing happily together. It was as though I had been transported back in time to a strangely familiar and beautiful place, far, far away in the mountains, where the colour of skin had no significance.

This was my first introduction to my guardian angel. It was he, my friend and protector, who had spoken to me and shown me the vision in the cracked mirror. He had stepped out of the past from the images of familiar places and faces and I remembered that his name was Lamont. He had come as a spirit to join me and once more establish a long-forgotten relationship.

'Hello, Jacob. Jacob, where are you?'

It was my mother, returning home. She found me lying in the back garden. I had been sleeping, but when I came round I felt quite refreshed, elated and invigorated.

Sunday was generally considered a rest day. It was, however, the main day of the week for holding sporting events. One Sunday afternoon my mother was seated in her rocking-chair, knitting a crochet pattern from an old magazine. I joined her in the front room, marching soldier-like around its perimeter. I was showing off by reciting questions and answers I had learned from my catechism. I kept up this exercise for some time, changing direction to coincide with the change of question to answer.

Suddenly a shower-burst tore through a black patch of overhanging cloud and the light which had been shining through our front door was virtually blocked out completely. Glancing to my side I caught sight of a tall man with a broad figure, firmly planted in the doorway with his back to the room. The door was wide open; the stranger had not uttered a single word of greeting. Although my father was not at home at the time, my mother simply looked him over and continued knitting.

I followed my mother's example and continued marching and reciting. When the stranger had arrived, I was on the fourth verse of the twenty-third Psalm. I suddenly remembered the question asked of the High Priests by Jesus Christ, 'Whom seek ye?' I had an idea and made up a further question and response to tag on to the end of the Psalm. Without any hesitation, I continued my recitation as follows:

> 'Even though I walk
> Through the valley of the shadow of death,
> I will fear no evil;
> Whom seek ye?
> Rain says ye, thou shelter.'

I repeated this over and over again in triumph and when I finished, the stranger had vanished.

My mother called me over. 'Jacob, come here a minute.'

'Yes, Ma,' I replied as I gingerly walked across to her. I was made wary by the tone of her voice and so my approach was defensive.

'Ma, I didn't mean to be rude or anything . . . I just made the words up into a little song, Ma.'

'Wait a minute son, slow down a minute. Come closer and listen carefully. That was a heavy shower of rain, and if that man hadn't sheltered from it even for a short while, he would have got soaking wet and might have got ill. He was not very polite, but neither were you – and you are still a child. You must not do that again.'

My mother always treated her children with understanding, tenderness, love and affection, the like of which I have never experienced since that time. Her loving care and gentle guidance had a profound impact on my development that will never be forgotten. Her sympathetic reprimand has stayed in my mind ever since and serves to remind me of the love which only a mother is capable of giving to her child. There were fleeting moments during my childhood when the atmosphere she created in our home seemed to be almost sacrosanct.

6

Greater Interest at School Began to Emerge

It was not until about the age of seven that I really began to take an interest in my school life. I enjoyed the discipline and most of my subjects, especially arithmetic, geography and music. The village was set in beautifully undulating terrain. The school was toward the north on low-lying ground. A small river meandered lazily at the back of it, winding its way westward through a culvert beneath the Southern Main Road and on to the open sea. The Gulf of Paria was some 500 yards away.

In the playground we heard the squawking of seagulls. Throughout my time at the Pointe-à-Pierre Government Elementary school I frequently enjoyed the fascinating sight of their leisurely flight through the warm air, relaxed but vigilant.

Not far from the school a railway viaduct crossed the Southern Main road aslant and monstrous steam-engines never failed to create great excitement. They blasted out a warning whistle as they approached the viaduct and their trundling sound, while crossing the railway bridge, reverberated around the surrounding area.

The greatest excitement occurred when we were in the playground at school, during the harvesting of sugar-cane. Several overladen wagons were transported from the estate to the factory by rail. As they rolled across the bridge bits of sugar-cane became dislodged or were

39

broken off. We used to pounce like vultures on the sweetness and carry off as much as we could.

In the midst of this fracas, Harry would say, 'Hey, hey! Leave that, it's mine,' and would charge upon a rival but lose his footing and end up slithering down the embankment, his prized possessions strewn around him.

In the meantime, the massive engine would be gathering up maximum steam to ride the upward gradient to the railway station about one mile away. The puffing sound of the engine could still be heard and we used to stand and watch the thick black smoke, jerking out of the chimney to level off as a canopy over the trailing wagons.

I can still picture the sight of the entire length of the receding train, wearily wending its way up the hill and finally disappearing behind a curtain of foliage in the distance.

At about eight years old, I seemed to have been experiencing a sudden surge of moral and intellectual development. My appreciation of what seemed to be good, bad, or indifferent was confirmed by the casual expressions of friends and relations of the family. I did not know what it was all about, but was pleased that I was not considered as naughty as many other boys of my age.

As the second son of a family of five children, with my father out at work all day and my elder brother attending to the more responsible errands, I became chief assistant to my mother. So far as household chores were concerned, I was often praised for being very helpful and I was naturally delighted.

7

Sea Fishing

In the year 1917, my father was in the employ of the Government Railways as a plate-layer in the remote village of Pointe-à-Pierre, Trinidad, then a British colony.

To cater for the needs of a growing family, he decided to work part time in the evenings and at weekends as a self-employed fisherman. The acquisition of a fishing boat and the required number of fish pots then became his principal objective.

'Pa, I would like to go with you to cut the bamboo for the fish pots,' I pleaded from time to time.

These pots were made from mature bamboo trees, sectioned and then put together in the manner of basket weaving.

'Take your time, son, you're still a bit too young. . . .'

'But I'm strong enough, Pa,' I would say, flexing my muscles to convince him.

'Oh, you're strong enough all right, but it's a bit too dangerous for you in the forest. Soon I'll take you to a patch of bamboo near-by to give you an idea of what it's like,' suggested my father.

He was a very kind and patient man and that was his general approach to all issues.

It was a bright Saturday morning when my father suddenly said to me, 'Well, Jacob, you always wanted to help me fetch the bamboo for the fish pots and I've decided to take you this afternoon.'

Somewhat taken unawares, I hesitated. 'Oh . . . Oh, yes Pa,' I said, overjoyed with excitement.

'You are sure you want to come with me?' my father asked as though prepared to give me an option.

'Yes Pa, I'll get ready right away to be on time. I've been wanting to help you for a long time, haven't I, Pa?'

'Yes, you're quite right, and we'll be off this afternoon – there's no need to get ready so early,' my father remarked affectionately.

And so, armed with stick and cutlass, it was time for us to depart. As we proceeded into the woods, he warned me as he had done previously, about some of the dangers to guard against in the forest.

On entering the bamboo grove, he said, 'Listen, son. Don't walk too close to me. Stay a little way behind.'

I was feeling a little nervous. 'Why, Pa? Why don't you want me to walk close to you?'

'You can walk close to me, but not too close in case I suddenly have to beat off a snake or something quickly. You wouldn't be in the way, then, you see?' he explained.

I heeded his instructions and all went very well. And having helped in the collection of the bamboo, I wanted to follow the project through to the end. When my father was ready to begin work on the making of the fish pots, I paid close attention to everything he did.

First of all the bamboo was cut to the required length then split into halves with a cutlass. Thin wafer-like strips were cut from the split surfaces and fashioned into shape using a very sharp knife. A separate unit was plaited in the shape of a funnel and finally attached to the main structure of the fish pot. When placed on the sea bed in the selected fishing ground, the fish would enter through the funnel.

42

After my father had explained how to set up the fish pot, I asked him, 'But Pa, if the fish could enter through the funnel, why couldn't it get out the same way?'

'Ah,' he said, 'once inside, the fish soon lose track of the entrance. With so many holes about, they get confused.'

That was enough to satisfy my curiosity.

The catch of fish from my father's weekend exploits was always a source of great excitement to me and the whole family. It was eaten with particular relish when set at the table.

Fortunately for our family, my father and mother were enterprising parents – they were always thinking up new schemes to help cope with the ever-recurring demands of daily living. Within a short space of time, the proceeds of my father's weekend enterprise had enabled him to purchase a goat, a pig, three hens and a rooster. Together, they formed the nucleus of our family's livestock.

During this time, the exploration of crude oil in the southern districts of our island had revealed sufficient amounts to justify its refinement on a commercial basis. Pointe-à-Pierre was chosen as the site for the construction of a major oil refining complex. It was probably in anticipation of this forthcoming industrial development that my father started to embark on his weekend fishing trips and my mother to further her prowess in the art of baking and catering.

As my mother became more and more occupied with the household chores, I became more involved in relieving her of some of the tasks.

One day, when she was preparing to bake some bread, I said, 'Ma, I would like to make the sweetbread and the buns for you, and the drops as well, if you like.'

'Oh, thank you son, but. . . .'

'I know how to make them all. I've seen you doing them lots of times, Ma,' I said.

'I know you can make them, Jacob, but I think you'll find the tins too difficult to manage. And, of course, you cannot manage the oven.'

'Oh no, I didn't mean the oven part, Ma, just making the buns and sweetbread, I thought.'

'I know what, Jacob, I'll see to everything except the dressing. I'll leave that for you to do completely.'

I must have looked blank, because I did not know what 'the dressing' was. After a few moments of embarrassed silence, I asked her, 'What is the dressing, Ma?'

'Before you put the buns in the oven, you have to dress them. You know – the clipping that you do with the scissors all over, then the coating of syrup or honey done with a feather and you finish off with a sprinkling of brown sugar,' my mother explained.

'Yes, I know, I've seen you do that often. Why do you do that, Ma?'

'Because when the bread and the buns come out of the oven, the dressing makes them all look shiny and nice.'

'Oh, I see. I'll do that part for you then, Ma.'

And so I became involved in the baking and bread-making process, which was one of the first ways that the rapid development of the island came to affect our family.

The oil refineries were virtually on our doorstep and a vast number of the Company's employees from the village and surrounding areas journeyed past the entrance of our home, to and fro from their work. The ingenuity of my parents would never have missed such a grand opportunity.

A fanciful display of freshly-baked bread, fried fish and pepper sauce, together with an elaborate assortment of cakes, ginger beer and other home-made refreshments were temptingly placed at the entrance to our front yard.

Such inducements proved too much for the average passer-by to ignore. And within a short while my parents were amply rewarded for all their hard work.

Campeche Bay was the main bathing place used by the black people in the village. Farther south, about 800 yards away, the white folk had established their own exclusive bathing quarters. They had the facility of a bathing jetty which extended into the sea, to a depth which ensured adequate safety for even their most ambitious spring-board divers.

From their quarters, some magnificent speed-boats issued forth in flamboyant colours, skimming the choppy waters in their race to some distant horizon.

'Hey! Jonny! There are lots of racing boats out today,' I once remarked excitedly, 'Have you noticed?' I asked.

'Yes, I've seen them,' said Jonny calmly, adding with his usual complacency, 'And there'll be many more, too.'

Jonny was about four years my senior and was not only the best swimmer but also the best all-round athlete in the village.

After a few moments I asked him, 'Jonny, why are you expecting even more speed-boats, then?'

They were still flashing by to and fro about half a mile out to sea, when Jonny replied, 'The big Southern Regatta takes place in two weeks' time and there are always many more boats about at this time, out practising.'

'Oh, by the way Jonny,' and older boy called out. 'How would you like to race in one of those boats?'

'I wouldn't,' said Jonny sharply, 'I'd build my own.'

This exchange had fired my own ambitions. I decided there and then that I too could build my own speed-boat, if I wanted to. But first of all, since I was only about seven or eight years old at the time, I would start by building my own scooter.

Whilst some of us on the beach were admiring the purposeful rampage of the speed-boats in preparation for the annual Regatta, there were others who were more interested in the goings-on at the bathing jetty itself. They had devised a sneaky approach to get a closer look. The best underwater swimmer was assigned to the task.

He came back with glittering tales of rampant frolic and reported the findings of his close-up inspection to our 'Secret Service'. There was a cosy little hut cosseted between a landing stage on one side and the actual bathing jetty on the other.

The hyper-activity inside the hut was apparently aided and abetted by the liberal and willing hand of Bacchus and repeatedly spilled over onto the actual bathing jetty. The participants gave spectacular performances of acrobatic exploits in a state of explosive hilarity. With incredible zest, each individual, one at a time, dashed along the jetty and on to a spring-board, catapulted high into the air and, somersaulting, plunged headlong into the deep blue sea, to a tumultuous round of applause.

At length the activities of the 'Secret Service' became over-extended and were terminated by the threat of prosecution.

Among the numerous delightful experiences of my childhood, seine-fishing was one of the most exciting. This was an occasion when the fishermen of the village gathered together and spread out a long, deep net, with floats at the top and weights at the bottom, outside Campeche Bay. It frequently occurred during the school holidays.

Zest and youthful fervour played havoc with our emotions as school children. All children are the same in this respect, but here, where we all knew one another so well, the formation of rival groups was a foregone conclusion.

A great catch was expected that morning. The fishermen were expected to beach their trawl at around 10 o'clock, but with more than twenty-five minutes to wait, the beach was already packed with spectators.

Wild chatter and laughter filled the air and the screeching of children was as natural and familiar as the raucous squawking of the gulls who were waiting for the catch with equal expectation.

'Oh, look! There they are!' a high-pitched squeaky voice exclaimed.

'Yes! Yes! Here they come!' yelled another voice with the greatest conviction.

As the fishermen advanced towards the beach with their laden trawl, feverish last-minute discussions erupted at random among the crowd, as they jostled together for a better position.

'Mary, Mary, what you looking for today?' asks a friend.

'Sardines,' says Mary, 'They're Mum's favourite. She loves sardines, but I like crab and shrimps. How about you?'

'We're not fussy, my dear. Anything goes for us, we just love it all.'

There were cross conversations everywhere and everyone seemed to speak at the same time. Meanwhile, heartened by the sight of the fish in the net, the seagulls squealed and squawked all the more, whirling in frenzy quite low above the water.

Renewed excitement erupted as the fishermen guarding the shore began wading into the sea. Ponderously, they inched their way towards the advancing boats, threshing about and punching the water with both hands. This was the most effective way of driving the trawled fish towards the back of the net.

Suddenly there was a terrifying cry, a voice yelling out in horror, 'Shark! Shark! Shark!' It rang through the air, freezing all action. There was a death-like hush as glaring eyes scanned the surface of the water in vain. Then, once more, the voice of warning pierced the silence with devastating urgency, 'Look out! Look out! There it is!'

Someone was feverishly pointing at the menacing fin of the monster as it streaked toward the trapped fish we were about to encircle.

'Get out! Everybody out! Get onto the beach. . . .'

This brusque command from the leader of the crew signified the real gravity of the situation. The fishermen on guard doubled their efforts to drive the shark away. The crew of the boat were armed with cudgels and cutlasses, hooks and crooks, and anything capable of making a splash in the water, in order to deter the shark. At last their efforts were rewarded and the shark headed back out to sea.

Strangely, when all was said and done, and we were all safely back at home, the meal prepared from such 'laboured loot' always seemed to be especially delicious. My childhood impression of seine-fishing as a whole was that it provided great excitement, hilarity and camaraderie among the people of the village.

One of the most difficult operations was the transferring of the fish from the seine to the fishing boat. Even now I am unsure of the detail, but somehow they managed and I remember marvelling at the huge variety of fish which thrashed about in the bottom of the boat.

There were red fish, marwhan, crocro, mullet, grouper, crascadoo, herring and a number of shell-fish. Realizing that they were not of the same family, I couldn't help wondering how it was that they were all caught up in one fell swoop.

Every instance of seine-fishing revealed a different catch, each with its own particular mixture of fish. But common to all the experiences, were the charm, adventure, endearment and goodwill, which drew our community into its own tight net.

A close view of the fish in the draught net heightened my interest in swimming and one evening after the seine had been pulled in, I said to my father, 'Pa, I would like to learn to swim like a fish.'

'Oh yes,' he replied calmly, then adding, 'You'll learn to swim all right, but not like a fish.'

'Why not, Pa? . . . eh Pa, why not?' I asked.

'Because human beings cannot breathe under water.'

'Oh, I know that,' I replied smartly, then added, 'I tried it once by accident and it didn't work out . . . it hurt.'

'Well, there you are, you see. But I can give you a few hints on swimming. I saw you the other day, You were getting along pretty well, I thought.'

This last remark delighted me and with my father's help I soon became a capable swimmer. My father was thus rewarded for his efforts and the interest he had taken.

8

Domestic Necessities

In the very early days when I crept and crawled about, I soon became aware that I was rather close to the ground, or on the ground itself. Time went quickly, however, and I soon realized that several houses were built partly or entirely on pillars, depending on the slope of the ground.

In the majority of cases at that time, the ground floor of a house was synonymous with the ground outside, just raised a few inches. As such, I would have had a close-up view of the naked earth. This was the way of life in the tropics for poor people who lived deep in the country.

In cases where the pillars were sufficiently high, pots and pans were stored there and all the cooking was done 'under the house'. Apart from these facilities, makeshift easy-chairs and hammocks provided some means of recreation and relaxation.

Quite often the entire area under the house was made habitable by enclosing it completely. Doors and windows were installed as necessary, and the proud owner advanced in social standing with his two-storey house. Such an undertaking was invariably achieved by the generous assistance of friends and neighbours and other members of the community. And so an ideal situation for the distribution of labour often occurred.

The material for the walls, and frequently the floor as well, consisted mainly of earth, cattle dung, wilted banana leaves, straw and grass. When mixed with water to the required consistency, the material was used as though it were concrete.

Groves of bamboo trees were in abundance in nearby forests, and their resilient stalks were capable of a wide variety of applications. They were sectioned and used to make baskets, fish pots, fans and fencing.

Bamboo was also used as an essential component in the construction of houses. Pillars and posts, struts and sills were all made from bamboo. The wall partition was built by forming a matrix of bamboo and then covering it with the earth, cattle dung and straw mixture.

The rendered surfaces of floors and partitions precluded the occurrence of cracks and crevasses. Thus, spiders and scorpions, cockroaches and centipedes, and other insects were left with no ready-made haven.

Community life in the village was centred upon the general well-being of every one of its inhabitants. There was a strong bond of common interest since everybody seemed to know everyone else and, in one way or another, were related.

The following is a brief example of the community spirit at work. There was an occasion when my father was contemplating doing some major work on the family home. It was no secret. He kept putting it off because his best friend was heavily engaged in some urgent matters. Then, out of the blue one afternoon, Mr Bobby called in to see him. My father was in the front garden.

'Hello, Geebee, you didn't tell me, but I heard,' said Mr Bobby to my father. Somewhat puzzled and surprised, my father hesitated.

'Didn't tell you what? I don't know. . . .'

'Oh yes,' interrupted Mr Bobby, 'You're about to expand, aren't you?'

'Ah, but that's no surprise; everybody knows my wife is

in the family way, and if everything goes well we'll have a larger family,' said father.

'That's the point,' said Mr Bobby sharply, 'and they know that you're preparing to expand the house . . . that's what I really came to see you about.'

'Oh yes, of course, of course,' replied my father with appreciation and delight. 'I had so many things on my mind, I hadn't got round to telling you personally. You know how things are,' added my father in apologetic tones.

Mr Bobby, middle-aged, full round cheeks and bushy eyebrows, was somewhat docile in his demeanour. He had offended my father a few weeks previously. His approach to my father was on the matter of offering a helping hand. In the circumstances, it was his manner of atonement.

His inhibitions brushed aside, Mr Bobby cleared his throat and said, 'Look here, Geebee, I'll come straight to the point: I have a good idea of how you're getting on with your preparation, so I've been rounding up the chaps. Any time you say the word, we'll be ready,' Mr Bobby concluded.

'Well, Bobby,' said my father, 'this is a very pleasant surprise,' he added as both men, smiling, shook hands heartily and were reconciled.

There and then they arranged for the work to begin in a week's time and at the agreed time the men began arriving, all free to help themselves to food and drink lavishly laid out on a long table in the yard. The group of mainly friends and relations were joined by a few men from a neighbouring village. Dividing up into groups, the men worked virtually non-stop over a weekend, beginning early in the morning and carrying on until the early hours of the next day.

That was the normal course of events which clearly demonstrated the nature of the community spirit in the village of Pointe-à-Pierre during those early days.

Such undertakings frequently transformed a single-roomed house on the ground floor to a two-storey building during the course of a single weekend. The actual finishing, of course, was done at their leisure by the family concerned.

During the post-operative discussions which generally followed such undertakings, a curious observer made a critical remark about my father's choice of roof covering for our reconstructed family home. Corrugated galvanised iron was the chosen material.

'You know, Geebee, to tell you the truth, I can't see why you decided on iron roof,' remarked the observer. He paused and looked around at the audience for support. He then continued, 'You see, the iron roof gets so hot, especially in the height of the dry season. Believe me, you can fry an egg on it,' he asserted in a priggish manner.

'Thank you, brother, I see your point. I have no reason to doubt you because I have never tried to fry an egg up there. Moreover, my Missis has enough frying pans in the kitchen anyway,' explained my father.

There were restrained chuckles and some downright laughter.

Within moments, my father raised his hands to draw attention. 'Let me tell you the main reason for my choice of roof. I left school at the age of seven and travelled the length and breadth of the country, living and working on sugar-cane and coconut plantations from time to time. The number of roofs I saw on fire put me off. I will not run the risk of my family getting burnt to death,' my father concluded.

That solemn declaration evoked a corresponding death-like hush. The silence lingered on.

Suddenly, cousin Minto sprung to his feet and said, 'Let me tell you a story about a straw roof. . . .' Just then a

53

few children in their early teens began gathering for their own party scheduled to follow the open discussion on the family accommodation.

'Ah, cousin Minto is going to tell a story!' exclaimed Hilda, a young 'belle' of the village. 'Can we listen to the story, Cousin Minto? Is it a true story?' she asked, with charm and affection.

'Yes, certainly, my dear. There are lots of seats – you can all sit down,' he said, pointing to the vacant seats.

Apart from being a village elder, Minto was a master story-teller. Very agile and quick of movement, he enacted the various parts of his stories with such realism and zest that his listeners were frequently moved to tears. He was a masterly evocator of dramatic tension and often created a charged atmosphere, which oscillated from pathos to hilarity, and vice versa.

'Now,' said cousin Minto, when the new arrivals were seated, 'I was about to tell you about a story concerning a house with a straw roof, but I must tell you of my brief experience during a visit to a house with a tin-covered roof. Of course, it was a long time ago. Do you want to hear it?'

'Oh yes, yes,' was the vigorous response.

'Well, it would have been very rude of me if I had continued to refuse the kind invitation of a dear old friend to visit him, and worse still if I had refused to enter his house. He was somewhat isolated.

'It was the height of the dry season. The sun was burning through the metal roof. All windows and doors were open, of course, but I was suffocating. Not being able to stand the heat any longer, I said to him: 'Jaffa, shall we go outside for a minute?'

'Well, you see, I suspected my uneasiness was causing him some concern. Well, that suggestion about going outside was the last straw.'

There was a pause. Then suddenly, Cousin Minto raised both arms in the air as though pleading for mercy from above and said:

'Jaffa had the most awful reddish eyes I'd ever seen. He approached me slowly and menacingly.

'How dare you, Minto? . . . You come to insult me inside my house! Get out before I pitch you out.' Jaffa was in a very angry mood. That was the last I saw of him.'

'But Cousin Minto, Cousin Minto!' exclaimed a voice from the back of the room. 'If the house was like an oven with the tin roof on it, then the straw roof would be much better, because we have a straw roof and it's not like an oven,' said the boy from the back of the room. The audience hummed with appreciation of the lad's reasoning.

'Ah, wait a minute. Listen to the full story,' urged Cousin Minto. 'You see something must have been wrong with Jaffa for quite a while.

'He was always in a great hurry. He built his house himself. The walls which supported the roof were too low, and with the roof almost flat, he was bound to have an oven on his hands. But that was a very long time ago.

'Nowadays,' Cousin Minto explained, 'with much higher walls and a roof with a good slope, the situation is much better. And quite apart from the risk of catching fire, let me tell you of some other incidents against the straw roofs.'

In accounting one of his experiences he explained that while lying in bed during a heavy rainfall at home, the straw roof of their house sprang a leak, several leaks. Armed with a bucket, he placed it on the wet spot on the floor. As if to annoy him, the dripping water abruptly changed location, only to change again as he tried to catch up with bucket and pans.

Cousin Minto went on to explain that it was not only

the difficulty in finding the leaks, and repairing them, but the fear of accidently setting it alight was also ever-present. In addition, he further explained that the thatched roof was always, and will continue to be an excellent playground, hunting ground and nesting place for many poisonous insects and even snakes.

'Gosh! Snakes as well?' someone in the audience remarked in awe. His roof was of straw.

'Oh yes, I assure you, and I shall tell you now of the gruesome experience I suffered as a little boy. I very rarely relate this story to anyone because it tends to frighten me all over again. Would you like to hear it?' Cousin Minto asked.

'Yes please, please, if you don't mind this time, we would like to hear it,' Hilda pleaded.

The request was agreed and Cousin Minto began. 'Let me remind you that I was a small boy, about four years old, but the incident was so terrifying, that being so young it made a lasting impression upon me,' he cautioned as he cast furtive glances toward the roof directly above his head. Many followed suit, wide-eyed.

He explained that it was in broad daylight when he heard the sound of an unusual rustling in the thatched roof of their house. He was alone in the house at that moment.

'Oh dear, insects . . . fighting again, or birds perhaps. Perhaps a big bird trying to steal some straw to build a nest, or something,' he said to himself.

With an expression of apprehension, Cousin Minto went on to explain that the rustling increased. It became frantic, and then he heard squeaks and squeals like a terrified mouse, muffled in the jaws of a playful cat, taking its own time.

He became so alarmed that he kept his gaze riveted to the centre of activity in the roof covering, but stood clear to one side in case a scurrying scorpion or a black-back centipede were to overrun its mark and tumble out of the straw and on to the floor.

The flurry intensified. It became more frantic. The squeals and squeaks grew louder and louder as the whole commotion moved waveringly down the slope of the roof. Suddenly, there was a forcible rupture, and all went quiet. But the rupture exposed the glistening greyish-white under belly of a huge snake. Only a small portion was exposed, but it was sufficient to gauge the size of the reptile as it remained pulsating, pulsating. . . .

Now stricken with terror, Cousin Minto continued to explain, he shouted to his elder brother: 'Jonathan, Jonathan . . . a big snake! Bring a stick! Quick! Hurry! Hurry!'

Jonathan, only two years older than Cousin Minto, was only a short distance away in their front yard. He immediately rushed into the house to see what it was all about. No sooner had he glanced up and seen the pulsating object protruding through the jagged fissure in the roofing, than he bolted back outside in terror. He was shouting, 'Papa, Papa, come quick. Quick – a big snake in the house is bulging from the roof.'

Both parents were in the back garden, but the urgency of Jonathan's announcement brought them promptly to the scene.

Cousin Minto's father had an alarming aversion to snakes and insects of all kinds, and the mere mention of 'snake' had a paralytic effect upon him. But here he had to protect his whole family. In preparation for such an eventuality, Cousin Minto explained that his father always kept a long sturdy forked rod in a particular part of his bedroom. Thus he was ready for the fray.

His father and mother had a quick glance to locate the exact position from which their attack should be launched. Just then the snake moved further into the straw to minimize its vulnerability.

His mother gasped, muffled her scream and backed away unsteadily. His father, greatly alarmed, dashed into the bedroom, scrambled for his forked rod, as he ordered them to stay away in the far corner of the room.

At this stage, Cousin Minto plunged deeper into the story and acting it out as principal witness and participant in the drama, continued, 'Within a moment, my father bounced back into the room. My mother, Jonathan and I were already huddled together in a corner. I tried to keep an eye fixed on the snake.

' "Who removed the rod from the usual place? Someone removed it! I can't find it!" said my father with rage, as he looked at Jonathan and me accusingly. He was very shaken and confused.

' "Stay there, you two! Don't move, you hear me?" my mother said to Jonathan and me as she hurried off into the bathroom. My father, with eyes trained on the roof, tiptoed furtively supposedly assessing the method of attack.

'Within a few moments my mother returned with the forked rod. My father, in his anxiety, had looked in the wrong corner. In any case, he didn't find it.

'Taking over the leadership at this stage, my mother said, "Jonathan, bring the little table for your father to stand on. Hurry!" My father was spurred back to reality. No doubt he had worked out the mode of attack, for he wasted no time in placing the table in the most suitable position.

'Immediately, my father hopped upon the table with an agility that took us all by surprise. Armed with the forked rod, he paused, steadied himself, then slowly took aim.

' "Quick Papa, quick! Don't let it get away," my mother shouted as the snake moved slightly.

'That rush of anxiety bothered my father somewhat,

and in reasserting himself, the rickety table suddenly developed a terrible wobble.

' "Oh dear, dear!" my mother exclaimed, and told Jonathan and me to keep the table still for our father.

'My greatest worry now was that I seemed to be directly on the spot where I believed the snake would fall if caught in the fork. I tried to change places with my brother, but he must have had the same thing in mind.

'Now with my father feeling more secure, he took a fresh aim. With accuracy of thrust, the body of the snake was firmly wedged between the prongs of the fork and pinned against the roofing.

'The snake made some frightening and chilling noises which echoed all over the room.

' "You've got 'im, Papa; don't let go," I shouted. And that was the general form of encouragement,' explained cousin Minto as he stared up at the roof, wide-eyed with cowardly stance, symbolic of imminent disaster.

As far as I could recall, Cousin Minto's father was in a very perilous situation. The encouragement from his family was stupendously impelling, and he braced himself to finish the job. Suddenly both ends of the viper broke loose from the thatched roof, coiling, untwisting and recoiling at the top of the forked rod, held secure.

'Move away! Go to a corner! Keep together!' were the sharp orders given by Cousin Minto's father to his family, as he struggled to maintain his balance on the increasingly wobbly table.

Mother and two sons darted to a far corner and huddled together gripped by fear and tearful. In hysterics, they shouted words of encouragement.

'Push Papa, you've still got him. Push harder Papa, harder. . . .'

Now, in great desperation, the snake seemed determined to make its descent, by wrapping itself around the rod.

This new tactic caused a new wave of anxiety. A desperate appeal from his wife, cloistered with their two sons at a relatively safe distance away, fittingly evoked a desperate response from her husband. A mighty thrust rent a huge hole in the roof, and through it both viper and fork disappeared, leaving the rickety table in a shambles. Beside the shambles, prostrated, was Cousin Minto's father, smiling.

With all the praise and admiration which may be showered upon a great conqueror, his family rushed to his assistance. It was a natural response to the love and affection, by which the entire family, and many others like it, were securely bound.

In the illustration, Cousin Minto had fully vindicated my father's choice of corrugated iron in preference to the thatched roof, and in so doing, my father was further credited as a man of wisdom and foresight.

Fortunately, I have not had such a gruesome experience. Nevertheless, being of a much younger age than I was at the time of the incidents he described, you will be able to judge the impact made upon me by the ordeal I am about to relate. My case was also a family matter . . . of a delicate nature.

Like most families living in remote parts of the country in the early days, a major call of nature, by convention, generally took us well beyond the rear boundary of our garden.

As a child, I seemed to enjoy the peaceful atmosphere cloaked in mystery and secrecy, in a sort of no-man's land. There, in quiet isolation, sheltered from the direct rays of the sun, and from humanity, the lush foliage offered a warm haven. Frequently one was pleased by the beautiful song of a high-flying acravat or chaffinch as they passed overhead on their way to some distant feeding ground. There, of course, several black birds, blue birds, yellow and several other types of birds frequented the bushes in energetic pursuit of fruit and insects at their feeding time.

Sudden confrontation with the human species awkwardly poised in their favourite retreat, often sent them darting off in a hectic frenzy, leaving some of their beautiful plumage entangled in a matted mesh of bushes.

Life in those bushes was active and varied, and so full of interest that one occasionally paid a penalty for being unwittingly distracted from the main purpose of one's visit. The penalty was always self-inflicted by the inadvertent use of stinging nettle leaves as the substitute for what came to be known as toilet paper. The penalty was devastating, never to be forgotten.

Despite the cosy atmosphere of a haven full of the amusing theatrical antics of birds and bees and all manner of insects in the dry season, the dripping damp foliage in the rainy season was endured with unbridled repugnance.

And so, in time, my father built a cesspit in our back garden, with floor boards and a box seat with a hole on top. All this was enclosed in a shed with a real door, as I explained it to my school mate friends at the time. It was a blessing for the whole family. Soon, however, it came to light that the water table in the locality was far too high to facilitate the customary posture for which the box with the hole was intended. There was no peace of mind. We were, of course, protected from the elements above, but very vulnerable from below; and the situation was at its worse during the rainy season. At this season, no matter how agile one might have been at manoeuvring, one never escaped the wrath engendered by the germ-laden upsplash of water on one's most tender parts. Household protestations brought about a speedy change.

During the construction of a new cesspit on much higher ground, my elder brother said to my father, 'But

Pa, you're making this one exactly like the first one. The same thing might happen again, wouldn't it Pa?'

'No, son,' replied our father. 'It won't happen here.'

'But Pa, why . . . why won't it happen here?' my brother asked, somewhat puzzled as to why it shouldn't.

'Well, you see, the ground is much higher, and the water level being much the same as in the first place, it will be much further below the ground up here,' explained our father, who seemed pleased about the interest my elder brother and I had shown.

Indeed this venture had put an end to the water problem. But, about six months later, a new unsettling occurrence came to light. I first became aware of it one afternoon when I was comfortably seated over the cesspit in the new little house on elevated ground. At first I heard a ticking sound, then it changed to a scratching or crackling sound, barely audible. Immediately, the frequency increased and so did the audibility. All this outburst of enthusiasm abruptly arrested the purpose of my visit.

Intense scrutiny led me to the source of the activity. In desperation, I sprang to my feet to confirm my suspicion. And peering through the hole in the seat, I saw a shimmering action all over what was supposed to be the walls of the cesspit. Like intricate patterns of silken tapestry, giant cockroaches in a perpetual shimmer, jostled one another for eminence or a vacant spot on the over-crowded walls of the cesspit.

With vivid notions of an invasion of those detestable creatures creeping up towards me on the box, in their antagonistic mood, I hastened to report the matter to my father. My mother had already informed him of the situation and the necessary steps to eradicate the menace had been taken. In those days the rigorous application of smoke and disinfectant was the most effective means of treatment. In this respect the family's problem had been overcome.

9

Bonzo and Lizzy

The livestock which my parents brought up from its
simple beginning, when my father embarked on part-time
fishing to augment the family's requirements, had indeed
flourished. And at about eight or nine years of age I
became familiar with attending to poultry, pigs and goats.
I was very interested in the care of the animals and
became more and more fascinated by the observation of
their characteristics. I made some illuminating discoveries, which, later on, I realized were equally applic-
able to human beings. While my palms hardened by the
extra work in keeping the animals well fed and watered,
my heart, on the other hand, seemed to have softened
somewhat. This may be seen from the following incidents.

At feeding time my attention was frequently drawn to
two cockerels. They jostled each other constantly; one
trying to push the other aside. They often made two or
three circles as though glued together . . . and all this for
an extra grain of corn. I always felt sorry for the one that
was pushed around. He was the weaker of the two. My
intervention would have disrupted the whole feeding
process.

A similar behaviour applied to pigs and goats, and I
dare say many other animals. But here, I shall give an
example of Billy and Meggy. They were Suzy's first litter.

Within a few days of birth, Billy set out to deprive his

sister of her quota of 'mother's milk'. Thus, he jostled her off her nursing nipple and took it over discarding that which he had already chosen. Meggy, unable to regain her position, took on Billy's cast-off. But Billy immediately switched back, pushing his sister off balance. I felt very sorry for Meggy and eventually intervened by restricting Billy. I physically restrained him for short periods in order that Meggy should have her fair share.

Suzy was a very kind and attentive mother; and from her behaviour, I believe she was in sympathy with Meggy. She yielded a copious amount of milk, and after all, she knew there would be enough to meet all requirements, I concluded to myself. Some time later, as circumstances would have it, this kindly animal was subjected to a traumatic incident which upset me terribly, and involved my parents, friends and neighbours alike.

It was my responsibility to look after the animals at that period. On this particular occasion, I'd tethered Suzy to a sturdy guava tree in one of the best grazing fields in our locality. On my return to fetch her in the evening she was nowhere to be found. The sun suddenly embarked upon a rapid descent. A disquieting load from nowhere dropped upon my shoulders with a heavy thud; and immediately yoked me up. Like a bumbling buffoon, I found myself groping around, mumbling, fumbling and stumbling along paths, with which, but a moment ago, I had been absolutely familiar.

Inadvertently, I came across a path which loomed larger than the rest. In my predicament, I followed it and within moments, I was back home safe and sound. My heart had floated out of its thoracic cage and remained in suspension at the back of my throat for quite a while. Immediately, I flopped down on the settee gasping for breath, suffocating. My mother had sensed the danger. With great anxiety, she hurried towards me. I was perplexed and tearful.

65

'Jacob, my boy! What's the matter, son?' she asked with deep concern. 'Come, let's go into the kitchen,' she said with extended arms as she approached me on the settee in the hall.

My mother's voice had a wonderfully consoling effect upon me. Furthermore, it was as though my roguish heart, in fear of being shamefully admonished, had retreated to its natural habitat, totally subdued. My mother was going to support me . . . my anguish had disappeared.

'Tell me, what's the matter, my boy?' asked my mother, soothingly.

'It's Suzy, Ma; Suzy is missing. I'm sure Ma, quite sure . . . she's not where I tied her, Ma,' I insisted as I became tearful once more.

'All right, Jacob, I believe you, my son. Everything will be all right. Your father will soon be here. I'll explain, so try not to be so upset,' whispered my mother softly as she patted me on my shoulder in her efforts to console me.

Within moments my father arrived. My mother broke the news to him immediately and forthwith, he organised a search party. I now had renewed hopes of having our Suzy back, and her characteristics began to impress themselves anew upon me. She was a tall brown goat with long black legs, ears, and an intelligent-looking face; a kind, very attentive mother with a remarkable milk yield. She invariably responded to her name on purposeful calls. With all that information about Suzy, added to the fact that I was the only person who knew exactly where she was put to graze, made me an important member of the search party.

With flambeaux, rope, cutlass and all the necessary paraphernalia, the party of six was ready to set off and my father told me to take them to the spot where the goat was tied. It was about seven o'clock in the evening and pitch-dark, but the area was amply illuminated by the surfeit of torchlight.

I felt as though I was on a great expedition and likened myself to Christopher Columbus on his third voyage to the Caribbean in 1498. Indeed it was my third visit to the area, since it was I who tied Suzy there in the first place.

'Tell me, son, are you sure this is the right track?' my father asked, raising his flambeaux high above his head.

'Yes Pa, I'm quite sure this is the track.'

'Where is the tree you tied her to? How far is it?'

'Not far, Pa; it's just at the back of this guava patch,' I replied, quickening my steps.

On arrival, I directed my father to the particular tree. The party fanned out.

'That goat might have been set free,' someone remarked.

'In that case, she could be anywhere by now,' responded another.

Just then another member of the party called out, 'Here we are! . . . The boy was right. Well, not exactly, but near enough. There is the mark on the tree where the poor goat was tied,' said the observer, giving me credit for my directions.

My father patted me on the back in appreciation. 'I say let's split up and have a good search around. She knows your voice, Jacob, so keep calling. She's bound to be nearby,' remarked my father.

'She might have got tangled up somewhere, Pa, otherwise she would have gone home,' I said to my father. He agreed.

I kept up an incessant call: 'Suzy! Suzy! Where are you . . . where are you, Suzy?'

At last there was a positive response and we all went to investigate. Suzy was haunched up, all four legs tied firmly to trees in the most pitiful manner. All the party were relived of course and expressed their indignation at what had occurred. There were muted mutterings among some of the men, but I was not told anything, except that it was the act of some cruel person.

A few months later, one of Mr Pocock's prize ewes suffered a similar indignity. Mr Pocock, a portly, imposing man, one of the better-offs in his sixties, lived in a fairly secluded area in his cottage attended by maids and other helpers on his property.

In fading light one late afternoon, there was a great uproar unusually close to the cottage. The sudden and doleful howling of a stray black mongrel dog in Mr Pocock's back garden had sent shock waves through the region. Lizzy, a wide-eyed hysterical maid at Mr Pocock's cottage, hurried across to a window on the first floor to locate the howling dog. Stunned by what she had seen, she lapsed into a fit of hysteria, screaming and shouting: 'No! No, Bonzo! . . . No, Bonzo . . . It can't be. . . .'

Muttering, she sank to the floor, partly rescued by Edna, her junior and more robust assistant.

'What's the matter, Lizzy? Are you all right?' Edna asked.

'Yes, I'm quite all right; I just felt a little faint . . . that stray dog howling like that,' remarked Lizzy, clearly at great pains to conceal the facts.

Now on her feet again and about to walk away from the scene at the window, Edna tried to jog her memory: 'Lizzy, I think I heard you mention Bonzo's name, do you remember. . . ?'

'No, no, I don't remember saying anything or seeing anything . . . I just kept hearing that howling dog, howling, howling,' Lizzy said.

Just then Mr Pocock arrived, and seeing Lizzy somewhat unbalanced, suggested that she should retire to her quarters for a while. She was Mr Pocock's long-trusted maid, unmarried in her late twenties with a nervous disposition. Her medium height and slim build were the principal assets of her attraction.

The stray mongrel, renowned throughout the village for his wanton ramblings, instinctively gave chase to the intruder. Indeed both dog and human (Bonzo) were intruders and startled the wits out of each other. The result was a rebellious howling protestation by the former and a desperate flight by the latter, stumbling and falling over himself to avoid being recognised. Hurriedly picking himself up, the stooping, gaunt figure scurried away through the fencing, across a deep cart-track and into an adjacent cane field.

But, like the cascabelle, a venomous snake which always returned to the scene of a disturbance, the stray dog returned to the area almost immediately with a renewed burst of howling, much more doleful than before. This was no 'sleeping dog' by any means. There was no letting up. The curious goat/human posturing with which the dog was confronted must have thrown him into a state of perplexity, with which to grapple in the manner of his seasoned peculiarity.

As in Suzy's case, the legs of Mr Pocock's goat were tied and haunched up with a similar type of cord. The renewed howling had brought Mr Pocock to the scene. Forthwith he carried out a thorough investigation into the matter. He was exasperated, and was determined more than ever to uphold his reputation as a dauntless avenger and firm believer in the strict administration of the law. Being a man of immense influence, there was no telling what lay in store for Bonzo.

On recovering from her dizzy spell, Lizzy realized that she had identified Bonzo and that Edna, her much younger assistant, would not hesitate to inform Mr Pocock that she had mentioned Bonzo's name in her mutterings. In the circumstances, Lizzy realized that she, Lizzy, would be a principal witness, and as such, would have to give evidence against Bonzo. She was in a dilemma.

On the other hand, Bonzo knew that Lizzy had recognised him and that she would be obliged to attend the courts, and that the effects upon her would be devastating. Apart from all that, he did not relish the idea of a long-term imprisonment. He therefore decided on self-banishment and took to the forest for a life of seclusion.

News of Bonzo's plight had spread throughout the village and it was not until two years or more had elapsed that I came to know who Bonzo really was. I had seen him occasionally on the beach or while walking along the street. He seemed quiet and pleasant; and I was saddened by the thought that he had run away to live among snakes and dangerous animals.

At the periodical village meetings, Uncle Jimmy, the most influential village elder, often expressed his concern for Bonzo in his isolation, and now he was prepared to do all in his power to have him rehabilitated. Thus, at a special meeting he made a rallying call for support towards that end.

'How do you propose to get him back, Uncle Jimmy? . . . Moreover, he may not want to come back here to live,' said a member of the audience.

'Well, I've taken all that into account; it's now three years since his departure from the village. I think he has suffered enough . . . and let me tell you about my personal feelings for Bonzo.

'I knew Bonzo as an orphan from birth . . . born and bred in our community. I saw him grow up as a quiet, peaceful and respectable lad. I also saw him time and time again at many of our social gatherings trying to befriend both boys and girls of his own age. In one way or another, they shunned him and belittled him.'

Uncle Jimmy paused for a moment and glanced across the audience as though to identify the culprits. There was a fleeting air of discomfort among those who considered themselves guilty.

Continuing his observation, Uncle Jimmy went on, 'I tell you fellow villagers, I saw those things happening before my very eyes for quite a long time. Certain girls in particular scoffed at him, even in public places I tell you.'

Here again there was a pause. There seemed to be a moment of quiet reckoning. Then he went on to explain that the whole community must share some of the responsibility for Bonzo's plight. He said that in view of the circumstances, he personally, would arrange for Bonzo to be rehabilitated.

Someone in the back of the audience raised a question, 'But Uncle Jimmy, it's about three years since he ran away. Would he like to come back here? Where's he going to live?'

'I've taken all that into account,' replied Uncle Jimmy. 'Furthermore, I've already spoken to Father Romano; he is in full agreement and will help in any way he can,' concluded the venerable Elder.

No one knew the forest as well as Uncle Jimmy. He decided on the particular phase of the moon and day of the week. He fortified himself against the evil forces, known and unknown, alleged to roam the dark depths of the dense forest by day and night and set off one morning about an hour before dawn. As the light of day approached, the undergrowth bristled with nocturnal life as the various animals busied themselves, scurrying off to their respective sanctuaries.

The dry season was specially chosen, of course, and Uncle Jimmy had made considerable headway into the depths of the forest by late afternoon. In a small clearing he sounded the region, hooping a well-known hoop, then listening; hooping and listening attentively, he kept on and on. At length a slight rustle occurred among the bushes nearby.

'Bonzo, Bonzo is that you? . . . Bonzo, where are you? I'm Uncle Jimmy; I've come to see you.'

Only partially emerged from the bushes and heavily bearded, Bonzo very cautiously posed the question, 'Is it really you, Uncle Jimmy?' This was immediately followed by another question: 'Did anyone come with you, Uncle Jimmy?' Up to that time Bonzo was still very apprehensive. With such obvious expression, Uncle Jimmy assured him that he was the Uncle Jimmy who knew him from babyhood. He also assured him that he came alone. With that assurance, Bonzo advanced towards the centre of the clearing. With outstretched arms, both men greeted each other with an effusion of warmth and cordiality. At that moment of realization, the atmosphere seemed sacroscanct.

Following a brief spell of recovery, Bonzo was told of the arrangements that were being made for his rehabilitation; and that the whole idea was supported by the Parish Priest and all the influential people, and indeed the whole community.

It was further disclosed that he could be accommodated at Uncle Jimmy's home if he wished. Bonzo's eyes sparkled with great delight. He had always held Uncle Jimmy in great esteem – like a kind father – and believed in whatever he said. Thus, Bonzo agreed to return to the village. During the discussions which followed in the interim, it came to light that Bonzo had developed an astonishing sense of awareness, clarity of thought and understanding, seemingly well in advance of his contemporaries.

Bonzo's return to the village was in some way reminiscent of the Prodigal Son. Uncle Jimmy arranged a welcome party at his home, open to all who were willing to attend.

'Hello, Lizzy, are you going to the party on Saturday?' asked Jenny, one of her closest friends, smiling perkily.

'Don't know yet,' she replied.

'Don't know yet? And today is Thursday already? I understand he's quite a changed man, more developed, clever, and everything,' Jenny remarked with a touch of airs and graces.

'So what?' observed Lizzy, somewhat ruffled and on the defensive, for everyone knew of her involvement in Bonzo's case.

'Er . . . I suppose you'll be going to the party,' Lizzy asked in her timidity.

'Oh yes, my dear; I won't miss that for anything. I am a bit excited already. Everybody says he's a new man altogether; and besides, I can't let Uncle Jimmy down,' Jenny concluded.

Jenny and Lizzy were in their late twenties, contemporaries of Bonzo, who were all at school together, and they were still single. Lizzy quietly reflected on Jenny's remarks and exclaimed to herself: 'Oh, I see what she's up to!' Then she concluded that if anyone should have priority over Bonzo, then it was she.

With that resolve, Lizzy decided to attend the party and to assert herself in every way to attract Bonzo's attention. Thus, in a blazing attire of surprising elegance and good taste, and with all timidity brushed aside, she made a bold entrance to the house and joined the party.

She was greeted with considerable warmth, partly due to her sparkling appearance and partly due to the fact that her past involvement in Bonzo's case no longer affected the good community relationship, which had been assiduously engendered over the past few years.

Whilst slowly inching her way through the crowd to a refreshment table, a familiar voice called out, 'Lizzy, Lizzy.' It was a voice restrained but full of excitement. As she turned in the direction, her eyes and Bonzo's met. With fixed gaze, they advanced slowly towards each other, they paused very close to one another, searching deeply into each other's eyes, totally oblivious of their surroundings.

Jenny was only a few yards away and had heard Bonzo's call to Lizzy, and had witnessed the effects of the interaction of their approach towards each other. In that meeting, Jenny perceived an air of solemnity, far too precious and delicate for her to intervene.

During the encounter at the party, Lizzy and Bonzo spent most of the time together in an amicable relationship, no doubt trying to catch up with recent events. Bonzo had borne no malice whatsoever and during the ensuing weeks, a marked familiarity sprung up between them.

In the circumstances, Bonzo informed Uncle Jimmy of his desire to marry Lizzy if she was in agreement.

The following remark ensued, 'You know, Bonzo, marriage is a serious affair; are you sure you want to get married?'

'Yes, I'm quite sure now . . . to Lizzy. Of all the women in the village, I always fancied her the most.'

'All right then – what about her? Does she feel the same way about you?'

'I think so, judging from our conversation at the party. I will suggest it to her and if she agrees, I'd like to be engaged right away and get married as soon as possible,' Bonzo remarked in all seriousness.

'Well, in that case, let me know how Lizzy feels about it; then I'll have a chat with both of you before consulting Father Romano. You know that's how it's done,' observed Uncle Jimmy, beaming with smiles of approval.

Bonzo was delighted and full of jubilation. He hurried over to Lizzy's home immediately and informed her of the developments. It was mid morning. Lizzy was quite overwhelmed at the prospect. She stood frozen to the spot, bright-eyed and head tilted as though she could not believe her ears.

Gradually, a smile emerged, accompanied by a flood of tears. Thus cheerfulness and tearfulness coexisted in close harmony. Standing close to her, Bonzo proceeded to dry her tears with his handkerchief. She held his hand and stopped him. Reaching up and kissing him on the cheek, she quickly drew back to continue mopping her tears.

After a brief recovery, Lizzie said, 'You must excuse me, Bonzo; I'm so very happy. I fully agree with your proposal. Let us meet at the usual place on the beach tomorrow afternoon, so that we can have a quiet talk.'

Bonzo was delighted and returned home directly to report to Uncle Jimmy.

Immediately after Bonzo's departure, Lizzy's head became flooded with thoughts of motherhood, and as evening approached some daunting prospects began to surface. She pondered over fragmented statements of the marriage vow: '. . . to cherish . . . to have and to hold . . . till death. . . .'

The last two words raced round and round in her head, then slipped down to her neck. There they became transformed into millstones gyrating, faster, faster, faster. . . . Tormented by the thought of diverse conflicting issues, Lizzy screamed and rushed into her bathroom in a profusion of cold sweat. A fleeting glimpse of herself in the mirror abruptly arrested her attention. She paused to stare and stare, and to question . . . to question herself in depth.

She moved close up to the mirror; composed herself as best she could and then in her relaxed state, began the process of self analysis, looking deep into her own eyes as reflected in the mirror before her.

'Tell me,' she said, 'am I the said Lizzy, who took up the cudgel in a tiff with Jenny at Bonzo's party?'

From the reflection in the mirror, came the following remark, 'Yes, of course; you are the very same. You are concerned about not being married and not having a man to share the many virtues of life. Moreover, because of past events you believe that you have some priority over him. And you were prepared to fight for him. Good for you . . . a man admires a spirited woman. Marry him,' was the conclusion.

The following day, hours before her rendezvous with Bonzo on the beach, Lizzy reflected upon her fantasies of the previous evening. Unwittingly energised into a state of excitement and sexuality, she raced back to her dressing-room, and stood before her full-length mirror.

'Oh, I know,' she said aloud to herself, 'judging from the way Bonzo looked at me at the party, I'm sure he was impressed by my appearance . . . I'll wear the same dress,' she concluded.

Lizzy got changed immediately and, taking a hurried appraisal of herself in the mirror, she was delightfully surprised to realize for the first time how attractive her black skin appeared . . . glistening with health.

She was reluctant to concede that her velvet-looking brown eyes were so pleasantly set beneath crescent-shaped brows, that they curled upwards at their distal extremities. She had not observed, either, that when she smiled, cute dimples adorned the corners of her mouth, radiating a feeling of benevolence, affecting even the least sensitive. With Bonzo added to all that, Lizzy considered herself fortunate.

At the rendezvous Bonzo was patiently waiting and greeted her with a warm and affectionate smile.

'Well, you can't imagine how pleased I am that you've come,' said Bonzo as he advanced to meet her.

'Why? Did you not think I would turn up?'

'No, it's not that,' replied Bonzo briskly. 'You see, I'm not quite used to all this and it's difficult to believe that it's real; that's all.'

'Well, at any rate, Bonzo, I am real; I can tell you that without any doubt,' Lizzy assured him as she glanced at him with her most winsome smile.

'Oh, I saw that from a distance, especially with that dress; it suits you beautifully.'

'I'm very pleased thank you,' Lizzy responded and then there was a pause.

'You're thinking, I see. What about?' asked Bonzo as they walked arm in arm leisurely along the beach.

'Yes, I've been thinking very seriously about the marriage vow, where it says, "to hold and cherish and so on. . . ." '

'Yes, go on,' urged Bonzo.

'Well, I've been wondering whether you really care for me that much,' said Lizzy in a very subdued manner.

'Tell me, Lizzy, what's really bothering you?'

'It's about that night . . . that night when I was walking home alone in the dark. You pulled me into a bush on that lonely stretch of road, remember? You ripped off my skirt and tripped me over onto the ground . . . and then you ran off and left me! Why, Bonzo, why? . . . Why did you run off, if you cared for me so much?'

'Wait a minute, Lizzy! Listen, listen carefully, please I always wanted you, and I wanted you more than ever then . . . even now, but you were calling the police . . . and I didn't want either of us to be involved, that's all.'

'Look here, Bonzo, I didn't shout for help, did I? . . . I didn't. . . .'

'But you kept shouting all the time. . . .'

77

'Bonzo, Bonzo, try to understand; I was very excited and perhaps a bit noisy. I couldn't help it. So, when I thought of that again last night and began to get excited all over again, I began to wonder whether you really love me. Do you understand, Bonzo?'

'Yes, of course, I see your point now. I hope you appreciate my explanation also,' Bonzo concluded.

At the height of their discussion, they had stopped walking and stood face to face to elucidate a point. When the issue of the past was finally clarified, they were standing facing each other. They consolidated their affairs with a brief hug and a kiss. Their first hurdle had been overcome.

Now with contented hearts on their leisurely homeward stroll, the ecstatic resplendency of a full moon in a cloudless sky provided a romantic atmosphere, exquisitely enhanced by the exotic perfume of the highly scented 'flowers of the night'. They floundered, then placing their arms around each other and tightening their grasp, they were in jubilation. The purpose of their rendezvous had been achieved.

To everyone's delight, their engagement was announced in the village church within three weeks and their marriage followed immediately.

In due course, Bonzo and Lizzy became ardent supporters of the village cricket club and rendered valuable assistance to its upkeep, particularly with fundraising projects. As a gesture of appreciation, the club gave them two complimentary tickets for the latest venture – a grand bus excursion to a popular seaside resort on an Easter Monday.

As the three buses set out from the heart of the village, where several visits to the rum shop were being made, the bus drivers jokingly drew attention to the time scheduled for departure. The hired band of musicians seated in the leading bus struck up the latest calypso music.

A tumultuous ovation erupted; those intending to travel hurried on board as the onlookers waved and danced to the music. Many who were unable to go on the excursion stood waving limply to the fading sound of the music in the distance.

The lure of a beautiful beach with crystal-clear water gently and rhythmically lapping the sandy slope was far too enticing to resist in the blazing sunshine. And so a swim, or a paddle, or a splash was more or less the routine indulgence.

Bonzo and Lizzy were in their bathing clothes, wading hand in hand in shallow waters. Gradually they veered away from the crowd. Glancing at their playful and affectionate behaviour, one could not help feeling that they were enjoying, after all, a well-deserved honeymoon bliss.

Suddenly, a raging storm rose up out of the blue and, in the twinkling of an eye, a mountainous mass of foaming water washed over their heads in their isolation, whilst a swirling wave, like a gigantic scythe, converged with the overhead umbrella of water and bungled them up completely out of sight. The swiftness of that devastating tragedy had consumed the senses of all concerned. Speechless figures, remaining still, wondered whether it was all a mirage.

In coming to terms with the facts, their sole consolation was that:

'The return to the fold of the LOST sheep in the forest had resulted in the end, to two HUMAN HEARTS being inextricably united.'

10

Sugar-cane Harvesting – Sidelights

On the whole, life in our village was full of happy moments, generally carefree and very delightful. A variety of recreational activities such as cricket, rounders, kite-flying, bird-catching, rowing, swimming and the occasional football game were among my principal hobbies during my childhood. As such, the opportunity for developing a healthy and sportsmanlike relationship with others was ever present.

On special occasions such as Sports Day, main interests were focused on athletics and donkey racing, and events such as three-legged races and the egg and spoon race provided great fun and laughter. Harvesting of the sugar-cane, in its peculiar way, also provided a great deal of excitement, especially among the children.

Proper cultivation of the land necessitated the provision of furrows in order to ensure adequate drainage, and this seemed to be an essential feature in respect of the sugar-cane plantation for the production of maximum yields.

During the period of prolific growth, the less attentive, or the less capable, neglected the overhanging weeds and bushes at the furrows, and so, unsuspectingly, one occasionally stumbled over a startled couple lying in close formation, partly concealed by the overgrowth.

There were, too, other trespassers who deliberately

made their rendezvous in some odd places on the plantation depending upon the nature of their particular escapade. The alarmed couple in the ditch, over whom an innocent trespasser or a farmhand inadvertently stumbled, were invariably propelled into a state of acute embarrassment.

In such instances implications of blackmail were occasionally supplanted by a pledge of secrecy . . . by Good Faith. Whatever the compromise, life went on in its peaceful leisurely manner, and the village prospered from strength to strength.

Looking at a plantation from a distance, the flowering sugar-cane in full bloom, one was struck by the harmonious swaying of the blossoms in the breeze. On the one hand, they displayed a majestic beauty and discipline of a unique sophistication; on the other, they conjured up an expression of gaiety and leisurely abandonment. It may have been the latter attributes of the sugar-cane blossoms in full bloom, evocative of romantic notions, which enticed the amorous trespassers to the midst of the furrows. Even so, one would not have thought they would offer up their shadowy beds unreproachfully to man and woman, wild animals and snakes and insects, with equanimity.

During my childhood, the harvesting of the sugar-cane throughout that period was one of the most intensely exciting events, which began even before I started my schooling. There were cheers and shouts as the steam-engines laboured up each gradient with their overladen wagons of cropped product.

But when I grew older, I was able to visit the heart of the cane field and gave a helping hand on many occasions . . . pleasure, excitement and interest were all intensified. I was then an active participant and saw some extraordinary incidents, which seemed quite hilarious at the time.

During the transportation of the cane from the field to the factory, it often required the tact and skill of the donkey driver to keep his overladen cart on the go.

'We have ten trips to make today, Harry, so no playing up . . . you hear me?' Mr Coker said to his donkey on the approach to an up-hill gradient.

Harry, the donkey, pricked up his ears and emitted a muffled bray, but otherwise took no notice, for he was already wincing from the soaring temperature of the mid morning sun. Then, suddenly, he stopped as though to muster his resources for the formidable ascent. Threatening expletives charged the air in quick succession, and it was Gupta's timely intercession that saved both Mr Coker and his donkey from further vexation. Gupta, a wayward boy of about ten years of age, and his companion had waited furtively for this moment.

'Ah, good morning, Mr Coker, can we help? . . . Don't know if you want a hand,' said smiling Gupta.

'Oh yes, my son; bless you. You arrived just in time.'

'Just in time for what, Mr Coker?' asked Gupta with an expectant look.

'Oh, I haven't any sweets or anything like that. You see, I want to get in quite a few loads today, and my Harry here was just about to play the fool, weren't you Harry?' Mr Coker asserted as he directed his last few words of his remark to the donkey, with a touch of venom in his voice.

Time was the important issue for Mr Coker, but for Gupta and his companion, pilfering and hiving away the most succulent stalks of sugar-cane from the rear of the cart was their primary objective.

With Mr Coker at one arm of the shaft, pulling and directing at the top of his voice, Gupta pulling at the other arm, Harry, the donkey, firmly harnessed in his usual 'habitat', and with Gupta's companion allegedly helping from the back, the ascent to the summit was attained with thanks and praise from Mr Coker. This was a queer example of the effects of TEAMWORK!

11

Wakes: Tamboo-Bamboo: Stick Fighting

Quiet and peaceful as it was in my early childhood, our village was not exempt from the typical ups and down of community life. Here now, the normal serenity of our household and relatives had been interrupted by a matter of profound importance. Aunt Nenen, of whom we were particularly fond, had been in ill health for a considerable time and had taken a turn for the worse. Her deterioration was rapid and warranted constant vigil at her bedside. Despite the unstinted acts of devotion by many relatives and friends, the time had come for the administration of her Last Rites.

The Priest responded promptly to the call. He was deeply moved and did all he could to conceal his emotions. He failed but had kept trying to the end of his task, at which time he gestured the sign of the cross to Nenen on her dying bed and to the household, and departed without uttering a single word. The atmosphere was still and tense.

Immediately, there was a slight movement.

'Jacob! Jacob! Nenen wants you close to her,' a female relative whispered to me urgently and gave up the seat she had occupied at the bedside.

Immediately, there was a marked change in Nenen's breathing. At once I knew that she was about to die. 'I know all about deaths,' I said to myself, for I had learnt about the death of Jesus Christ and his burial. 'Nenen will rise up again if not on the third day, sometime later but she will. . . ,' I concluded, fully consoled in that profound belief.

I had attended several funerals before but I'd never been so close to someone who was about to die. I was nervous and very distraught. Instantly, however, a remarkable change came over me. It was a strange feeling. It prevented me from feeling sad. Being fully aware of the transformation, I sat up and paid closer attention to Nenen. I uttered a little prayer for her in my mind and thanked her for all the things she did for me. I was in buoyant mood, pleased with the thoughts that she would no longer have to do everybody's hard work.

Her belaboured breathing drew the attention of everyone in the room. It had a very depressing effect upon us all. I looked round momentarily and caught sight of my mother. She glanced at me through a half-open door. Our eyes met squarely. She looked at me fixedly – then calmly retreated, satisfied no doubt that I was in good spirits.

Nenen's breathing continued to deteriorate. I looked intently at the rise and fall of her chest, wondering how long it would last. She had had many sleepless hours, and her insomnia may have led her to stare ostensibly at a deep crack in the ceiling of the room which she often spoke about. Suddenly a dramatic change developed in her breathing; several people joined in prayers while others attended to less urgent necessities of the occasion. I had kept a constant watch on Nenen and was deeply saddened by her enfeeblement, and ultimately, by her silent departure from this world – I saw her take her last breath. Despite the expectation, it was as though time itself had momentarily stopped.

Then suddenly, a flood of anguish pervaded the entire atmosphere, hysterical at first then settled down to a form of sober lamentation at which stage all but a few seemed utterly drained of energy. Nevertheless, in the tropics at that period, the dead had to be buried as soon as possible in the absence of a refrigerator. The incident of death occurring at, say ten o'clock in the morning, generally necessitated arrangements for the wake to take place during the night and the funeral the following day. Hence quick action was taken in the usual way and Nenen was buried, leaving the entire community to mourn her loss.

News of the wake spread like wild fire through the village and neighbouring districts. By sunset, on the day of her death, scores of sympathisers had called at the home to pay their respects and were assured of the wake being planned for the same night.

At the appropriate hour the guests gathered in the largest available room prepared for the purpose. Several tables placed end-to-end or otherwise, chairs, stools, old soap boxes and the like – oh, benches too – accommodated the guests as they sat around the table singing their favourite hymns with unbridled gusto, selected in turn by request. This contrasted with the melancholic undertones of muffled wailing and weeping in the background, further saddened by the symbolic weeping – of candles too – with their feeble flame flickering with compassion.

Interspersed between spare hymn books on the table, decanters half-full on the table with intoxicating beverage cast their irresistible spell at random, inexorably claiming victims one by one, slowly and positively in favour of 'Bacchus'. Hot strong black coffee lavishly served, seemingly energized the participants to sustain a sleepless night.

Meanwhile, along the street in close proximity, the tamboo-bamboo band was being primed, and they too were similarly served with stimulating beverage. And, as percussionists, their explosive beat and syncopated rhythms thundered through the stillness of the night for miles around. The gaiety of the tamboo-bamboo band contrasted markedly with the doleful atmosphere within the house; but such was the tradition for it was firmly believed in some quarters that such rejoicing was an expression of happiness for the release of the deceased from the suffering in this sinful life.

As a child, while pondering over the implications of Nenen's death in the privacy of my mind, I realized how pretty the lighted candles on the long table indoors were to look at. Then my recollection of All Saints' Night (Halloween) emerged and I saw myself with members of our family, friends and relations helping to clear the cemetery of overgrown bushes and weeds prior to the grand spectacle of All Saints' Night. Identification of neglected graves occasionally gave rise to disputes which were always contained in fear of being haunted by ghosts for disturbing the tranquillity of their resting place. I had thought that it must have been for that reason, too, that in those days one tended to whisper in a graveyard. In my mind I'd seen the outline of Nenen's grave. It was long enough and wide enough to hold lots and lots of candles to brighten her path to Heaven, so I thought, and was delighted.

The tamboo-bamboo band held for me an especial fascination, and since by posterity they played an active part in the celebration of wakes throughout my native country. I venture to throw some light, not only on their musical instruments but also on the general character-istics of the players with whom I had been personally acquainted during my youth. There was a remarkable peculiarity about the members. They were all men about the age of eighteen to thirty and lived deep in the interior of the country. They were not given to smiling easily and bore a marked resemblance to certain African tribes classified as warriors or mountain people as illustrated in some educational literature on the culture of some developing countries.

Their instruments were made of bamboo trunk (stalk) cut in different lengths to produce the sound of a required pitch when struck with a percussion stick. The diameter of the stalk or trunk played an important part in tone production. The disc (sometimes referred to as joint) of the section was generally punctured or removed completely, except the bottom one which was retained to contain a small amount of water which enhanced the quality of the tone.

A section of bamboo, say five feet long, would produce a deeper sound than a shorter length of equal diameter. Thus the longer sections were used as bass. Lifted up a few inches and dropped on the ground with a thud provided a strong beat while the much shorter sections with percussion sticks made a heyday of it all. The members of the band with the shorter lengths of bamboo usually squatted to form a circle within which singers and dancers showed off their prowess to the full.

The players of that particular band were noted for their calm temperament, physical fitness and their craftsmanship in woodwork and basketry. Then too, they were keen gardeners, accustomed to hard work and living from the produce of the land. Stick playing (stick fighting) was their favourite hobby at which their agility and dexterity were exceptional but, as I recalled, the leader of the group was in a class well above the rest. He was the notorious Katango.

Katango was well-known locally as the champion stick fighter of the area and was very rarely seen in action, preferring to reserve his appearances for combat during the carnival celebrations. He was remarkably fleet-footed and reputed to have a technique all of his own. In addition, he was completely ambidextrous and was able to whip his stick through his opponent with either hand like a flash of lightning at inconceivable angles.

Moreover, during the process of combat he frequently changed his stick-hand in the twinkling of an eye to press home his advantage with devastating results. Blood-stains, old and new from open head wounds of his adversaries, bore unnerving testimony of a rare and formidable contender.

12

Grave Lamentation

In our community, my parents were by no means singular in their approach to husbandry as a means of economic expedience. Our increasing animal stocks made it necessary for me to go farther afield in order to procure adequate feed supplies. Therefore, I often frequented numerous regions – some very remote – for example, neglected farms, groves, plains and prairies.

The quest often took on the appearance of an expedition, armed with cutlass, grass knife, rope and sack according to the type of fodder decided upon. The most popular were paragrass, hog's meat or pig's vine and sugar-cane tops (canetop) depending on the time of year. This form of outdoor activity, in addition to fetching firewood from nearby forests for heating the oven for the purpose of bread-baking by my mother, had begun to engage my attention in a small way well before I was nine.

Both my parents were keen advocates of good discipline, better education and self-improvement. We had a peaceful and contented family home. In the course of our normal affairs, suddenly it seemed to me as though time had taken a great leap forward; and I had turned eleven years of age.

As the Oil Company continued its development, more people were engaged in various categories of employment, a great many of whom walked past our house on the main road. The reputation of excellence in supplying refreshments to the numerous employees, who purchased their requirements from my mother on their way to and from work, had been long established. And now a new record was about to be set, with great delight for the whole family.

But, alas! At the height of her venture, fate dealt a cruel blow. My mother complained of feeling ill quite suddenly. As far as I can remember, it was a Sunday evening. She was in the habit of having an eggnog at that time. I usually prepared it for her.

She was in great pain, and thinking that the drink would help to soothe it, I asked, 'Ma, shall I make your eggnog for you now, Ma?'

Writhing with pain, she barely managed to nod twice, very feebly.

I felt very sorry for her and hurriedly prepared the eggnog with the hope that it would relieve the pain. But, in the emergency, my mother was driven off to the nearest hospital a few miles away. Her eggnog was untouched.

It was revealed later that my mother was in great agony throughout the journey to the hospital. On arrival the intensity of the pain was such that she pleaded mercifully to be operated upon for relief. The operation was performed. My mother did not survive the ordeal. She died at the hospital. I was eleven years, six months and six days old.

News of my mother's death swept through the village like a hurricane, leaving an atmosphere of gloom, confusion and desolation. The hearts of our family and relatives were torn apart with grief.

I was too young to evaluate the implications, but the numerous issues which emerged from my mother's death were magnified and compounded in my mind's eye. The wake and funeral arrangements were promptly executed.

So great was the impact that I appeared to have been in a state of partial amnesia for months and months on end.

I vividly recalled her loving care and affection for all members of our family; and my association with her during my visits to the Hot Springs and later, when a stranger who, sheltering from the rain, blotted out the daylight from our doorway. But, even so, my greatest sadness and indeed torment, was always aroused during recollections of my efforts to console her with her customary drink of eggnog, during those final moments of extreme anguish.

Even now, I see a veiled panoramic view of the sorrowful event; but strangely, I do not recall her countenance, and despite my concerted efforts to obtain a photograph of her which may have been taken even when she was a child, I have not been successful . . . so far.

Immediately following my mother's death my father obtained the assistance of a helper. She was kind and motherly but at no time was she considered a substitute for my mother. However, she did relieve our household of a great deal of the confusion which inevitably emerged, particularly with regard to the laundering of our clothes. My father retained his employment with the Railways Authority.

13

Tales of Gupta, Kasi Kojo and Simoko –
DOMESTIC

In the course of events life in our family adapted to a new order. My father was obliged to devote most of his time to his work which kept him away from home for considerable periods of time. I was thirteen when a delicate issue arose. After pondering a great deal over the matter he decided to entrust me with the task of discharging this important errand.

'Jacob, come here a minute,' my father called to me. I was just outside the front door and he was seated at a table in the hall. It was the same hall I had tramped round when I was reciting my 'Whom seek ye . . .' catechism much earlier on.

'Yes Pa,' I responded as I advanced towards him at the table.

'Come . . . bring a chair and sit down,' he said quite calmly. I moved a chair up to the table and sat down as instructed.

'Now son, you're growing up well and I want you to do a very important job for me. . . .'

'Oh, good. . . .'

'Wait a minute, I haven't told you what it is as yet . . . now, listen very carefully. Do you know Gupta?'

'Yes, Pa, one of your Indian friends; you were talking to him last week, I think.'

'That's right, that's right,' replied my father with a smile of content. 'Well, on Saturday morning I would like you to take Isabelle to him. He'll keep her in his pasture for a few hours then hand her back to you to bring her home.'

'I will do that, Pa, but . . . is the grass on his farm better than the grass she is getting?' I asked curiously with the feeling that I was at fault with regard to her feed.

He hesitated, then said quickly, 'Oh no, no son, it's not that. You see, Isabelle wants to be a mother with a little calf of her own. I believe Gupta's bull would be a good father for her calf. Gupta thinks so too, so we decided they should get to know each other for a little while,' my father explained.

I was very delighted and began to see myself taking care of the baby calf straight away.

My father cautioned me about the dangerous aspects of the errand, particularly while leading the animal for a distance of a mile or more through rough land, and valleys. Isabelle was a heifer of pleasant disposition and she was well-accustomed to my handling.

I arrived at about 8 o'clock on the morning in question. Gupta was on the lookout and welcomed me on my approach to the track.

'This is a nice cow you have here, I don't suppose you had any trouble with her on the way here, had you?'

'Oh no, good old Isabelle was as good as ever.'

'What's her name? . . . Isabelle?'

'Yes, that's right.'

'But she's not old, in fact she is quite young. Your father explained everything to me. I'll lead the cow to the pasture,' he said, then called out to one of his sons to take me to a veranda in the farmhouse overlooking a fenced enclosure nearby.

Gupta had led Isabelle round to the back, unlocked a

big gate to the enclosure in which he set Isabelle free. I gathered that the enclosure was the pasture. Gupta immediately re-locked the gate and returned to the farmhouse.

The enclosure seemed about 200 feet square and Isabelle appeared to be the only living creature in it. Instantly, however, I discovered a shadowy object lurking in a remote corner of the field. Very gradually, the shadowy object took the form of an enormous gruesome black bull, motionless but disturbingly alert, with all attention focused on Isabelle. Fearing that she would be no match for such a huge animal in a fight, I turned my head away for a few moments. But my concern for Isabelle's safety prompted me to cast another glance in her direction.

The overtures of the animals had brought them clearly into view from the veranda. I was nervous but I steadied my nerves. At the height of their heated acquaintance-ship, the bull suddenly unleashed his pent-up energies in quasi leap-frog manipulations. The breath-taking pheno-menon compounded, blotting out a vast proportion of the skyline.

'Run, Isabelle! Run! Run!' I caught myself shouting to the astonishment of my hosts.

I was soon put at ease by all concerned – Gupta in particular.

On my homeward journey, I pondered over the whole affair and reflected upon similar frolics among cats, dogs, roosters and hens and a host of incidents, but nothing so disconcerting. It was, however, a matter of necessity.

* * *

One of my greatest delights was to listen to stories told by an elder of the village in the company of other children

95

and members of the family, usually in the evening. This practice has been observed so frequently over such a long period of years that I seem to have an endless list of folktales. The incident in respect of Gupta's pasture explained above reminded me of Kasi Kojo's predicament and a folktale in which Sipio and Madam Simoko are protagonists. Both are briefly described hereunder, narrated by Kasi Kojo himself.

* * *

Kasi Kojo's manner of narration always held us in suspense, and frequently in awe, as children, and although we may have heard the story several times before, we dared not say a word lest it be taken as an expression of disrespect. He was quick to point out the similarity of any daily occurrence with matters which had caused him some anguish in the past. In doing so, he would rise to his feet and with a noticeable change in his voice, pace the floor in his slow deliberate manner like a caged tiger back and forth.

Relatives or friends nearest his age would try to pacify him, and Toby, a sensitive, timid, black mongrel dog, would furtively depart from the scene, glancing sideways towards Kasi Kojo. His anger would rise considerably before there could be any appreciable appeasement. Had there not been the intervention of pleading voices and coaxing hands at times, such agonising may have been rather more lengthy.

In many ways, he may have equalled or even surpassed the Master Story-Teller, but by no means would he have had the audience, for no one would have run the risk of adding to the anger he would have already generated within himself, of his own accord. Coughing, sneezing or smiling, would have had to be a stifling affair, and certainly Toby, the dog, would not have risked staying around. In his later years, a notable sign of danger was the commencement of his heavy breathing prior to discarding his seat. And there was no effective concealment of his distended blood vessels on the ageing throat and forehead when his emotions were aroused. This is said with all due respect for it's a phenomenon which attends us all should we live long enough, I dare say.

Once Kasi Kojo had got going, he couldn't resist the temptation to relate the incident which had caused him the greatest humiliation of his life. As a child he was tall, and rather a big boy for his age, it was said. In fact, he grew to be quite a big man, tall and sturdy. He was among a group of smaller boys of his age, who were chased away from a mango tree in Mr Hector's garden. Raiding various fruit trees by a group of boys was a regular feature, but on this occasion Mr Hector had recognised them and yelled out their names as they fled. They were all local boys and everybody in the village knew each other.

Three days went by, then out of the blue Mr Hector called at Kasi Kojo's home and lodged a strong protest against him. As soon as Kasi Kojo set foot in the door that evening, he received a sound hiding from his father. Later on Kasi Kojo found out that none of his companions had been called to account and, indeed, no complaint had been lodged against them. As a result, he was the only person who was punished. He considered this most unfair and informed his father immediately, who in turn went over to Mr Hector, taking his son with him to clear up the matter once and for all.

Mr Hector, a thick set man of mixed blood – Negro and Indian – had seen their approach well in advance through his peep-window, and awaited them patiently, more furious than before.

'That's him! That's him!' Mr Hector explained,

broadening his chest as he tried to add to his five-foot stature in preparation for a showdown.

Kasi Kojo's father, a much bigger man, explained to Mr Hector that he had come in peace, but was somewhat bothered about why his son should be blamed and not the other boys as well. Feeling totally disarmed, Mr Hector dropped his shoulders, lowered his voice and advancing very close, explained that he was not really concerned so much about a mango or two, but it was about the foul, dirty business that was done and left right at the foot of the mango tree just where he normally stood to climb it.

Kasi Kojo (the child), sensing his father's fury and disgust, hurriedly protested, 'No, Papa! not me, Papa!' and adamantly disclaimed having anything to do with that.

The sincerity of the protest made his father think again. So he asked Mr Hector if he actually saw the boy on the spot . . . how did he know that it was his son? Pleased with his clever deduction, Mr Hector declared that the matter was quite simple, because judging from the size of what he saw, it was bound to have been the work of his son, he being by far bigger than any of the other boys.

'And don't argue,' he said, 'for it had taken me two whole days to work it out.'

Such was the nature of the humiliation Kasi Kojo had suffered, and there was no recourse to justice in those days.

Unfortunately, Kasi Kojo had several disappointments in the course of his affairs. Here is another incident: like most of the villagers at one time or another at Pointe-à-Pierre, he earned a living by fishing either full time or part-time. It was on an extraordinarily hot day when he had set out to sea. By 9 o'clock the scorching sun had begun to make its mark upon everything and everybody. As a result, he hurried from a profitable fishing ground, back to the nearby town.

His fresh catch had caught the eyes of several shoppers in the market and they gathered around his stall to make their purchase. Thus in a short while most of his fish was sold and he began to tidy up in readiness to return home to Pointe-à-Pierre. Just then a tall impressive man, passing by, paused and, seemingly pleased with the size and general appearance of the fish still on hand, offered to buy the lot, and it was sold to him except for one which had been reserved.

While collecting his belongings at the end of his work, on close examination he suspected that his prized fish had been spoiled by the heat of the sun and would no longer be fit to eat, despite the precautions he had taken. And now, he feared the consequences. Immediately, one of the regular hands at the market told him the Police Inspector who had bought the remainder of his fish a little while ago, was on his way back with a parcel wrapped with the paper served by him.

Kasi Kojo quickly made the sign of the cross upon himself and asked his friends and colleagues to carry on with their business as usual. He remained still, looking at a distant horizon. The Inspector entered the stall and slowly walked round, looking at everybody, in search of the person from whom he had bought the rotting fish. He paused at the door on his way out and looked back, but did not recognise the Elder. That incident had been substantiated by many of his colleagues, with astonishment. It made him somewhat of a mystic.

Kasi Kojo had long been regarded as a man of great faith with profound religious beliefs, and the fish market incident had strengthened the speculation and increased his status among his friends and relations in some inexplicable way.

The greatest misfortune to have attended him, however, was the disappointment and heartache he suffered by the alleged behaviour of the person he intended to marry. As far as I knew, it was a matter of infidelity on her part. He was affected by the incident to the extent that not only did he sever the relationship completely, but changed his way of life to that of a recluse.

He played the cuatro – a four-stringed instrument – with remarkable facility. No amount of appeasement, enticement or encouragement had ever persuaded him to believe that most women were loving and kind and certainly could not be exemplified by the behaviour of his ex-fiancée. Beneath it all, he was kind and affectionate with a vast reservoir of warmth for those he held in trust. I've had some quiet and lengthy conversations with him in my youth. I was not able to appreciate his depth of feelings at the time, but I sensed a particular rapport. The proof of this was seen from the fact that I was privileged to be entrusted with what I believed to have been some of his most cherished ancient prayers.

* * *

Behold! Once upon a time, deep into a tropical wilderness, burst forth a great big, black mountain which grew and grew to an enormous height, shrouded with thick dark-green foliage. The mountain became known as Phantama Grossa and was the scene of many strange happenings.

The village of Buccada which grew in its precincts was inhabited by strange people, but the strangest of them all was reputed to be Madam Simoko who was more than one thousand years old. She was known to live in a cabin, on the highest peak of the rugged mountain inaccessible to villagers. It was rumoured that she was once seen roaming through the foliage of the foot-hills dressed in jet black.

According to legend, the village of Buccada had been in the grip of her evil influence for generation upon generation, and the increasing occurrences of mysterious deaths, often of young children, prompted joint concerted action to protect the community from the foul deeds of the weird and wicked lady. She operated in the dead of night at a particular phase of the moon. Terrified observers believed that she descended from the mountain as a red big ball of fire to the foot-hills then on to the valleys and plains beyond, sucking the blood of her victims dry and returned to her cabin on the heights before the break of day.

At a special meeting of the village elders, Patrick Dickson whose only daughter, Sheila, was a victim three years ago, had just returned from an eighteen months' trek into the jungle in search of someone capable of assisting the villagers to avenge the death of his daughter. He had searched the length and breadth of the jungle, and at last had found the one man who was willing to take up the challenge. He was known as Slippery Sipio.

A man of slender stature, pointed face with darting beady eyes, exceptionally agile with a warrior-like temperament: stick-man, medicine-man, greasy and hairy all over, he seemed to fit the bill ideally. In any event there was no choice. Thus, Slippery Sipio was invited to the village secretly to study the ways of Madam Simoko.

During his months of preparation in secrecy, he had noted the numerous events on the occasions of her attacks. Approaching the hour of midnight, the dogs in the neighbourhood howled a most peculiar howl – their customary foreboding; and puppies and kittens and other pets awakened from their sleep in a state of frenzy.

At the stroke of twelve midnight by the clock of the village church in the valley, a red ball of fire was seen rising from the mountain top. The howling of the dogs intensified and finally subsided in muffled submission as the fireball floated down to the plains and petered out.

Each day during his months of preparation, Slippery Sipio anointed his hairy body with his appropriate repellents to counteract the evil forces of Madam Sinoko. He inched his way up the foothills to secure a vantage point at the right moment. He knew that she would awaken from her spell moments before her next attack, thus he waited patiently.

At the approaching moment, he heard the sudden scurrying of animal life, the desperate flutter of wings and the muted disquietude of fledglings. Immediately, the dogs began their howling ritual, and the clock began to strike the midnight hour.

Suddenly, an agonising scream pierced the mountain air and a red fireball, in a burst of fury, shot up from the cabin. Now stealthily, entering the cabin, Slippery Sipio began his search. At length he burst out into laughter – a laughter of success. He had found what he was looking for. Madam Simoko, like a serpent, had shed her skin in order to carry out her escapade.

From his sack of special ingredients, Slippery Sipio lathered the entire raw surface of the skin and departed. At length, a faint light appeared in the precincts of the foot-hills and ascended to the cabin. There was a deafening silence; then suddenly a maddening cry exploded in the cabin. Madam Simoko was unable to re-enter her peppery skin, and so, herself died a painful and most horrible death, lying in her blood-stained vomit.

As a result of their marvellous deed, Patrick Duncan was crowned King and Slippery Sipio was hailed the hero of Buccada and was feasted for forty days and forty nights. There were no more mysterious deaths. A grand celebration was held in the playing fields for all the children in the village; and the expression of delight on their faces filled the heart of every villager, for the children were now able to sleep at nights, undisturbed.

When the good news spread around, all the people of Buccada and those beyond the mountain and the plains around, heaved a heavy sigh of relief, setting off a great big gust of wind in the atmosphere which swept across the face of the earth and continues even up to this present time. Simoko's body had disappeared, but her spirit took control of the wind seeking vengeance.

Such was another tragic tale of long, long ago. Somehow, they tended to lighten the pressures of everyday life upon the various families in the village, despite their gruesome connotations.

14

Scooter Accident

Engulfed by the exuberant spirit of inter-village rivalry, I was elected to compete in a race against the champion of an adjacent village; everyone called him Mauro. He was a boxer, fighter in every way, a boaster and a cheat. Those qualities added to prowess as a scooter rider made him a formidable contender.

As the grand occasion approached, Harris, an enthusiastic promoter of about nineteen and a staunch supporter of the event called in to discuss the matter at my home; he was in buoyant mood.

'Hello Jacob, congratulations, man . . . you know you were elected – as the village champion – to take part in the inter-village competition. I'd like to know how you feel about it. Would you like to take part?' asked Harris, smiling in anticipation of an affirmative reply.

'I'm not particularly interested but I'd like to know how good my scooter is compared with his.'

'Ah, well; this is your chance to find out. Good, good! I'll put your name down and will let you know the arrangements in good time.'

'How long do you think it will be from now?'

'Oh, not long, now that I am certain you'll be taking part . . . well, I must be dashing. . . .'

'But wait a minute, Harris, I want to put in as much practice as possible so I'd like to have an idea . . . one week, two weeks or whatever.'

'Yes, yes, yes of course . . . look here; say two weeks at least. And listen! . . . For Heaven's sake, keep your eyes on Mauro during the race,' Harris cautioned seriously.

'Oh yes, I'll keep an eye on him all right. I am sure my scooter is faster than his, so all I have to do is to get an early start ahead of him and put my lookouts at the corners to give me the all clear signal so that I can hug in and prevent him from overtaking me.'

'That's a very good idea, Jacob, marvellous idea . . . but you all must be very careful with the traffic; it could be very dangerous. Well, good luck, I'll see you again,' Harris concluded, and departed well-satisfied.

The oil refinery in our neighbourhood continued its expansion and many of its employees moved into our village. Over a considerably short period, the population had increased enormously.

This, of course, applied to all the adjacent districts and many beyond. Sports and recreational facilities sprouted into existence everywhere, and a highly inter-village rivalry emerged.

Various competitions were organised, and cash wagers, cups, trophies and shields were the contested prizes. All such activities were carried out in an atmosphere of music and song. Youths and even children were automatically caught up in the rivalry which, looking back, often exceeded the limit necessary to maintain good relationships. I was about thirteen.

I believe my spirit of adventure had taken a few leaps since my mother died, for during the intervening two years, with my father away from home, at work for long periods, I indulged in all manner of sporting ventures, with an appreciable degree of success. I emerged as the champion home-made scooter rider of my native village.

The course was set on the main North-South Road,

105

with lookouts at every bend, the sharpest and most dangerous later named after my father, George Browne, was opposite the entrance to our front yard. It extended over a distance of about eight hundred yards, down the hill.

The steepest region as far as I could recall was situated at that sharp right-hand bend. At the appointed time, the race was off to a good start, amidst shouts of applause supported by our respective supporters, mainly youths. I'd taken a head start and was determined to finish the race that way.

On approaching the half-way point, which incidentally was the notorious bend at the front of our house, the 'lookout' appeared to have been waving me on frantically. Assuming that all was clear, I cut in on the curve while glancing back to assess my chances of victory.

I knew very little of what occurred between that moment and three days later. I collided head-on with a motor car, was knocked unconscious and taken to a hospital in San Fernando.

It was on the fourth day during the process of regaining consciousness that I pondered over the length of my fingers and scrutinized a scar on my left arm in order to identify myself, for myself. I did not know who I was, or what I was doing in that strange looking place.

News that I had died circulated through the village and had caused considerable anxiety especially among those who were likely to be judged, or held responsible in one way or another. Naturally, I returned to the land of the living. On the seventh day after the accident, I was discharged from hospital and taken home by train. I was met at the railway station by several close relatives.

Cousin Minto, the master story-teller, was among those who had gathered at the railway station to meet me.

Slowly, he advanced towards me, and closely examined

my bandaged head, then remarked, 'Look what you've done to yourself!' pausing as though I should look into an imaginary mirror somewhere to look at myself. 'If I was your father, I would give you a good cut tail here and now, to teach you a lesson,' he concluded.

I admired Cousin Minto as a very good story-teller, but not for one moment had I compared him, or anyone else, with my father. His remarks in the midst of so many of my well-wishers had grieved me deeply, and I trembled with shame and guilt as my bandaged head throbbed relentlessly. Instantly, in my mind's eye, I saw my Cousin Minto tumble headlong down to the lowest rung of my ladder of estimation.

Later on I realised how fortunate I had been, for I was told that bits of my brain were scattered all over our front garden as I tried to run away, as everyone had done, after the accident.

Without doubt, had it not been for the expertise of the doctor with whose motor car I had collided, the story may have been quite different. I was obviously in the wrong, and was saddened at not having had the opportunity to express my thanks and appreciation for the treatment I had received. My father was very understanding, to say the least. He had helped me back to a speedy recovery, without severe reproof. However, when the dust had settled, he cautioned me against the temptation of wild pursuits and daring in order to prove myself better than anyone else.

He ended his remarks by the assertion, 'And look here, son! . . . be careful who you trust.'

'Yes, Pa; I'll be careful,' I replied, holding my head low in respect, and in thought. My father was an excellent counsellor.

15

Storm at Sea

From time to time, everywhere, various towns and villages have had their share of communal distress in one form or another, and Pointe-à-Pierre was by no means an exception. On a sultry afternoon, before the onset of the rainy season, a distant intermittent rumbling of low intensity had had a disquieting effect upon the community.

'You hear that?' someone remarked alarmingly, toning down his voice to a whisper. The rumblings persisted and the alarm ran through the length and breadth of the village.

The great concern was due to the fact that the older folk or elders had heard some convincing unpalatable tales of similar occurrences in the past. The general feeling may have been intensified by the air of superstition which still hung over the village at the time, for it was not yet the season for a change of weather.

On the third day of rumblings, storm clouds began to gather over the village and blotted out the late afternoon sun. As children, we thought it was very exciting. There had been several storms occasionally, but somehow the nature of events on this occasion seemed unique. Some roosters must have thought it rather strange also, for with obvious apprehension they had signalled their brood to roost and stood alert, as hens do when protecting their chicks from a mongoose raid. Anxious fishermen kept watch as the clouds and rumblings persisted late into the evening.

In council, it was agreed that it would be better to set to sea the following morning. They knew that such weather facilitated their catch, and their fish-pots (fish-traps) dispersed in the fishing grounds some distance at sea, would be rather difficult to locate, should the stormy weather really set in. Not only would they be unable to sight their land marks, but the risk of losing both catch and fish-pots by surging undercurrents on the sea-bed was much too great to contemplate, and so with their torches, well before dawn, most of the fishermen, including my father, set off to sea from Campeche Bay – the very bay at which I learned to swim.

'What you think of this business?' asked a timid fisherman.

'Not happy! Not happy at all! But, I can't afford to lose my pots and catch as well.'

A bright and promising sunrise had cheered all hearts, but before mid-morning, a heavy overcast sky had crept back over the village and surrounding areas, with outbursts of lightning and thunder. High winds whipped up the waters to an alarming roar that echoed for many miles inland.

Everyone hoped that the village fishermen would have escaped the full impact of the storm or would have had time to cut inland to an adjacent village, and not proceed to the fishing grounds. Whatever the decision, there was bound to be some element of danger.

My father was always very cautious in such matters, yet I was deeply concerned. I think it was mainly for his sake, for he worked very hard to support the family, especially after the death of my mother.

Normally the men would have begun to return home at

about midday, but on that occasion there were no signs of anyone from the various lookouts on high ground along the beach.

As the position grew worse, with rough seas, high winds, persistent lightning and thunder, the church bell, typical in such cases, began its mournful toll, and everyone for miles around knew that the fishermen of the village were in grave danger. This was common practice.

Fortunately, many of the fishermen, sensing the danger on the way out to sea, had broken off their journey and headed for the nearest village along the coast. Others had risked getting to their destinations only to abandon all attempts at collecting their catch owing to the heavy seas. There were many, too, who could not even see or distinguish their land-markers, and those who had sighted the church steeple as their marker had had only very brief glimpses as the flashes of lightning had allowed. And furthermore, battling against winds and waves, and tidal currents, exacted a heavy expenditure of energy from everyone. And there were the single-handed fishermen, like my father, out at sea at that moment of horror.

My father had been in the habit of setting his fish-pots in two different locations, one of which was much nearer the shore, even though the prospects of a good catch were not usually as good as those farther afield, but this served him well when he was pressed for time.

Realising the potential danger in going further out to sea on this dangerous occasion, he attended to the catch in the location nearer land, and set back for home by way of the nearest village along the coast. His catch was surprisingly greater than usual, and he received an enthusiastic welcome there, mainly because he had survived the ordeal. He was well-known and was in the company of other colleagues who were waiting to brave the weather back home on foot.

110

When he did return home, some other children and I who were in a similar plight, were strung out along the beach with all manner of torches as the church bell continued its peal. It was only 5 p.m. but it was as dark as midnight on a moonless night.

On hearing that my father had returned safely, I edged my way out of the crowd very relieved, but still slightly sorrowful. Some women and children were sobbing aloud as I passed by. As soon as I was clear of the crowd, I began to run home to look for my father, but he was on his way to look for me. We met on the way. I ran towards him, and greeted him:

'Hello, Pa! I'm glad you're back!' I said, holding his hand firmly.

I accompanied him back to the beach, to join the waiting crowd. He was a kind man, and a small crowd gathered around him for whatever information he had about their loved ones. He comforted those who had not heard about their relatives and friends and assured them that in such weather no one would have taken undue risks. Fortunately, the storm petered off almost abruptly as it had begun.

My mother had died only eighteen months previously, and one of my greatest fears was that of losing my father also. It could well have been the case for there were rumours of two missing fishermen from our village. Their wrecked boats were eventually recovered on the beach only a short distance away from our favourite place. Other villages too had their share of losses and the incident was regarded as being one of the worst in the history of the region for many years.

Judging from the magnitude of the storm, it was considered miraculous that many more lives were not lost. A special Service was held. In all dealings with the community, the role of the church had been of paramount

111

importance to all, and here, in point of fact, its intercession had minimised our anxieties and restored confidence for the future.

16

Storm in the Woods

The provision of firewood for cooking or baking was an essential requirement in everyday life in our village, and I had been in the habit of collecting it long before the death of my mother. With that experience behind me, shortly after she had died, as usual, I set out into the woods on a routine gathering of brambles and firewood, with my cutlass. Although I knew the various weather signs as well as everyone else of my age – about thirteen – I must have lacked the astuteness of an adult, and was caught in the woods and thick bushes by what seemed at first to be a passing shower.

I knew the area very well, including every little deer track and those of the wild hog and other animals. But the heavy downpour of rain had washed away everything, and had laid a dirty blanket of water ankle deep and more, all over the region.

I searched eagerly for direction, by the nature of trees, their height or clearance, or overhanging branches, but everywhere began to look alike in the dim, damp atmosphere of the forest. I looked around anxiously, pondered and prayed, and called upon Lamont to come to my aid. Suddenly, I found myself advancing in a certain direction, making my own landmarks by cutting or breaking off branches of small trees in my path.

The lightning and thunder continued relentlessly, and

even the type of trees that had been providing some shelter at the earlier stages of the storm had now surrendered to the onslaught and the sodden foliage had begun to dispose of their accumulated store of water. Eventually I succeeded in working my way out of the forest, and on to a wood I vaguely recognised.

'There should be a ravine nearby, somewhere,' I said to myself as I stood, looking around, pondering. Immediately I responded to the impulse to proceed along the course I was following. I was now rather concerned and had quickened my steps somewhat. It was quite a heavy downpour.

Within a few minutes, I came abruptly upon a swollen ravine, lost a foothold, misbalanced and sprawled into the fast-moving, muddy turbulent water. In the process I let go of my cutlass for fear of injury to myself, and was swept along by the swirling torrent. I was now virtually in a 'river'. I had a good notion of the course of the ravine, for it was a well-known landmark. But the water had completely covered the normally visible objects of identification on its banks and cast some doubt in my mind.

In addition, it was a rather frightful experience to be swept away in a current tending to turn me around, rooting me away from overhanging branches, stubs and twigs, or anything I laid hands on in order to check my drive downstream. My mind now focused on a subterranean culvert which lay askew beneath the station road, about fifty yards away. I was desperate. Suddenly, a feeling of tranquillity came over me, and I knew that no harm would come to me if I kept on the lookout.

Drawing from all my sources of energy, I stretched out and caught hold of a stout branch of a guava tree, lurched myself out of the swirling waters and landed firmly on the muddy bank, strewn with long weeping paragrass and debris. The storm was over, and I was unscathed except for a few bruises over my limbs and body.

In that flooded ravine, the number of things that coursed through my mind had greatly taxed my childhood belief in the good nature of my Guardian Soul, Lamont. My escape from what I vividly imagined to be a yawning culvert beneath the road to the railway station, waiting to gobble me up, was yet another confirmation of my belief in protective agencies.

Many of the tales we were told as children were concerned with the sea, lakes and rivers; and one which stuck in my mind while being swept along in the water was the story of a great big bull that usually went for a drink each day in the cool of the afternoon. A gruesome beast, partly crocodile and partly serpent, had observed the ways of the bull, and lay in wait for him one afternoon, with its long tail firmly secured to the deeply embedded roots of a tree. The beast hid himself in a hole at the bottom of the lake.

He had long decided to match his strength against that of the bull, and was now ready for the contest. In due course, the lumbering bull advanced to the edge of the water as usual for his drink, but on this occasion he paused and looked round for a brief moment, as though with foreboding, before settling down for his copious intake.

Within a minute, the atrocious beast had sunk its vicious fangs through the nose of the towering bull, and a tug-of-war of immense intensity had begun. Several minutes had elapsed with both creatures being stretched to the limit, neither giving way. At length there was an explosion, and a rush of air bubbles burst through the surface of the water in the vicinity of the turmoil. The water was now deeply tinged in scarlet, and the bull had freed himself from the terrifying clutch of the water monster, now certainly dead.

The bull had stayed his ground, and cautiously inched

himself backwards to safety, none the worse for his experience. We were often told of lurid menacing creatures lurking beneath the surface of muddy waters, and such thoughts tended to pervade my mind while in the swirling waters of the ravine. I did not lose hope.

17

Hunting: Kite-flying: Aberrations

Hunting in our village was a sport, and to some extent, a necessity. Although I was somewhat curious, it did not appeal to me in any special way. I knew that such enterprises required a certain amount of daring, skill and ingenuity, and therefore I was interested in acquainting myself with the basic requirements for the task. I knew too that it would improve my knowledge of the wildlife in our environment and that I would learn about some of the greater hazards of the forest.

At about thirteen, I began venturing in a mild way in the company of trusted relatives upon whose guidance I was utterly dependent, for the pitfalls of night hunting in the forest were numerous and dangerous. I soon learned to recognise certain sounds and to evaluate the potential dangers. From the bark of a dog in the distance, I had learned whether the quarry had taken refuge in a tree or a hole in the ground. And in the latter case, I was further able to tell if some form of aggression had been encountered by the dog.

A fairly common occurrence was that a dog would pick up the trail of an agouti, a species of rodent. With the dog close on its tail, the animal would dart into a hole, flashing past an offshoot as sanctuary in which one of the most venomous of snakes known in the region would have been asleep. Having been so rudely awakened by the mad dash of the agouti which probably shared the same hole but different quarters, the snake would be in no mood to tolerate any further intrusion, let alone a barking dog. The inexperienced dog, or the too adventurous, therefore, would have met with almost instant death, in pursuing it to the entrance of the hole.

It was in such circumstances that the experienced dog, whether by scent or instinct, would, at the entrance of the hole, change the character of its bark. The huntsmen would at once realise the gravity and the urgency of the situation. I quickly learned to train my torch onto the target, and was able after a while to distinguish the animal or reptile by the colour or tinge in its eyes.

When an animal like the opossum was hunted and caught, there was always great delight, for it was a daring and callous raider of the chicken roost. During the hunt, it was usually penned up in its favourite fruit tree – golden apple – when cornered, the characteristic brilliance of its eyes reflected by the torch never failed to be astonishingly impressive.

The animals were hunted also for adding variety to our food stock and for the pleasure and excitement it gave to the enthusiasts or the skilful. In many cases, hunting was also regarded mainly as a sport and in this respect, the deer and the 'wild hog' were primary targets.

The deer, however, was usually hunted by the overseer of the neighbouring coconut plantations – a large estate situated at the north of our village in the district of Pointe-à-Pierre. The deer, as I recall, outran the average dog, thus several dogs were engaged in the hunt, and the overseer and his aides were on horseback. They were white people, better-off and therefore better capable of covering vast acres of land, sometimes for several days, in pursuit of their quarry, secure in their privilege to rampage across anyone's property with impunity.

The deer hunt usually took place during daytime; the hunting of the wild boar was also executed during the day. I believe, however, that there were numerous incidents of nighttime encounters as well. There were gruesome tales about the hunting of this animal, but I was left in a state of uncertainty on the whole issue, for I had not myself taken part in such dangerous adventures.

For example, as a child I was told that the wild boar was terribly vicious, and was noted for the ferocity of its counter-attacks. One story described a night hunt during which the animal at bay ripped an inexperienced dog to ribbons within seconds. The dog died a merciless death.

Another story described a similar instance when the animal, usually a loner, was hotly pursued by three dogs experienced in the hunting of this particular animal. Realising its predicament, the boar dashed for cover – to protect its rump – backed against a large tree trunk and made a stand for it, facing the enemies. Frothing at the mouth, it crouched tensely, in desperation, with full display of its protruding fangs, curved and glistening. The vicious and energetic beast, raving and grunting and charging back and forth through the arc of a semi-circle, was in deadly rampage for its survival.

The three dogs had fanned out along the arc, in their concerted attack upon the animal. The most experienced dog sought out the vulnerability of the boar then, instinctively interchanging their positions and mode, kept up a sustained harassment, until the animal was rendered utterly defenceless from exhaustion.

The eyes of all the animals I saw during a night hunt, when reflected in the torch light, showed a peculiar brilliance typical of the particular animal. Thus, in time, one was able to distinguish, to a great extent, not only the difference between mammals and reptiles, but some of the species as well.

The seasoned huntsman was versed in every aspect of the enterprise. From my point of view, the whole exercise of night hunting was potentially dangerous and was certainly not a pastime of my choice.

* * *

As a teenager, kite-flying was also one of my favourite pastimes, and the fighter-kite was my first choice. I usually preferred grey or pale blue tissue paper for covering over the framework which was made from thin narrow strips of wood, very light in weight and yet sturdy enough for the purpose. The stripped stem of the feather-like leaves of the mature coconut plants was most suitable for that purpose. The fighter-kite was diamond-shaped and constructed to fly with the diagonal of greater dimension in the vertical position.

The tissue paper was pasted to the frame with a suitable mixture of flour and water. It was provided with a controlling tail in very much the same way as at the time of writing. The tail, however, was fitted with thin flakes or splinters of broken bottle pasted in position at certain intervals.

The region of the thread nearest the kite was covered over with a mixture of ground glass in a suitable paste as part of its armoury, the tail being the main offensive weapon. By means of an appropriate attachment of the control thread or cord, to the body of the kite, a well-balanced performance was achieved.

In such a case, the kite easily attained a suitable altitude and remained virtually motionless in the breeze, and would hardly be seen because of its colour against a sky of similar background. Suitably controlled, the fighter-kite would ascend rapidly to a great height in a vertical line and would suddenly break off and go into a straight dive, breaking off equally abruptly to streak away either to the right or to the left, on command. In this situation, the head and tail assume a horizontal position. In all circumstances, the nature of the prevailing wind played an important part.

'Fights' were frequently arranged and the winner – the kite-flyer – awarded a suitable prize. In some instances, a stake would be put up and the whole affair supervised by judges and referees. A good fighter-kite on display was always delightful to watch.

There were, of course, many other types of kites and the best known of these was the 'Mad Bull'. It was usually hexagonal in shape and the largest of all kites that were made at the time. It was said to have lifted a child off the ground in a strong wind, and up into the clouds, never to return to the earth.

Other legendary stories revealed not only a child being taken into the clouds, but up and up and far, far away across deep and dangerous gorges and crevasses, ravines and rivers and lakes and lagoons, only to release its infant cargo very gently into the jungle.

'The 'Mad Bull' was constructed with a device which, agitated by the wind, emitted a weird sound like an enraged bull, or a wailing siren of some kind. Usually, it was bright multi-coloured and flew sedately, quite unlike the darting manoeuvres of the fighter-kite.

Despite the apparent calm of the 'Mad Bull', in the hands of a skilful operator, it presented a formidable threat to the fighter-kite from the point of view that it was constructed in such a way as to demolish the 'enemy', not by severing its flying or control thread, but by a method of ramming or harpooning, thus ensuring total destruction. Its massive weight, strength and course flying cord were backed up by its harpoon-shaped contraption on its nose. By themselves, they constituted an armoury of some significance. In addition, an extraordinary long tail, spliced with splintered bottle and glass as an integral part of its offensive weapon, made the 'Mad Bull' a fearsome adversary in terms of 'air combat'. It was likened to the fighter-bomber aircraft, whereas the name 'fighter-kite' spoke for itself. Despite the grand spectacle and attraction of the 'Mad Bull', I rather fancied the 'fighter-kite', many of which I had made and flown from time to time over a period of many years.

In my youth, my friends and I used to admire the 'dog fights' shown on the cinema screen, and I had always fancied myself as being a fighter pilot, completely ignorant of the abhorrence of war. It was strange, however, that despite the references to the machines of war, for the most part while flying my kite, I imagined myself to be up there with it, looking down upon the landmarks I knew so well.

I'd made a special note of Mr Edwin's garden, not because nobody knew the extent of his land, but because he was reputed to have 'ranged' it so that anyone who stole and ate the produce would become utterly sick and would be forced to seek his valued help, and so be identified.

Then, too, I would survey the region of our home from the air, noting well the sharp bend in the road. I saw time and time again the spot in our front garden where it was alleged that fragments of my brain were scattered on the occasion of my scooter accident. While flying my kite, I made up stories. But, to me, they were not really stories, for I saw everything from above, quite vividly.

In my imagination, I soared to greater heights with my kite as though I were part of it, and became quite concerned about the 'Dwen' stories. I tried to locate their secret hiding place on several occasions without avail. They frequented the dense forest it was said, while others believed that it was only deep in the jungle they could be found. But, in an instant, they could be all over the place. Many people in our village, and others from neighbouring villages, too, believed the stories to be legendary only, but every now and then some peculiar incident would occur to discredit that belief.

And, whenever the matter was raised, usually in the market place, a woman's voice would be heard to say, 'I tell you! There's no smoke without fire!'

And a reference would be made to the latest incident in which a relative of mine was involved.

Cousin Mato, middle-aged, stocky, with a wide knowledge of the forest, was in urgent need of some bamboo to replenish his stock of fishpots. He dreaded the region of Togo Woods, which bordered the far regions of the best bamboo grove, but decided to brave the situation.

On a bright Saturday morning he set off on his quest, as he had so frequently done. It was usually quite dark after six o'clock in the evening, and much darker still in the forest. At seven o'clock, when there were no signs of his return, an alarm was raised and a search party of about a dozen men with torches and dogs set out into the forest on their search for him.

They kept together at first, and 'hooped' their well-known 'hoop' with hands cupped over their mouths to project their voices. They hooped (called) and listened attentively, hooped and listened, and hooped and listened, as they wended their way deeper and deeper into the forest. But there was no response until at length a faint sound, hooping, seemed to emerge everywhere in the distance.

The group split into three and one of the factions reported a positive response which had brought some cheer and hope to their hearts. But this was short-lived, for within seconds the response had receded as far as it ever was, deep into the forest.

It was an established fact that the whooping sounds in the forest had lured experienced and knowledgeable men away from their tracks in daytime, let alone during darker hours. Armed with garlic, ointments and various oddities for warding off evil spirits, the search continued into the dead of the night. But on the hour of one o'clock on the Sunday morning, utter exhaustion had beset them. Doggedly, they cleared a small area and lit a healthy fire to keep at bay dangerous animals and venomous snakes. Secretly in their hearts, however, they believed that a healthy fire was the most effective defence against the invisible . . . dwens and ghosts which were thought to be synonymous.

According to legend the whooping in the forests were the cries for motherly companionship by the ghosts of still-born babies, and by those babies who had not yet been christened at the time of their death. There were many versions of the story, but that was the most authentic in my childhood days.

Two days and two nights had elapsed without discovering a single trace of my cousin Mato, but strangely, he wandered back to the village on the third day, weak, tired and somewhat absent-minded. However, he recalled having responded to whooping calls by someone in distress, he thought. He had eventually lost his way, and his memory.

In reality for me, kite-flying was a most evocative pursuit. At times the excursions of my mind seemed boundless. For example, in my bird's eye view from my kite while in flight, I saw quite vividly the strategy of the various motor vehicles of the day, in their manoeuvre to get to the top of the hill, as they passed our home. There were motor lorries with solid tyres, straining to get up the steep hill, and to negotiate the dangerous bend in the road where we lived. (That particular bend in the main road was subsequently named after my father: 'George Browne Corner'.)

In their attempt to ascend the hill, the least capable of vehicles, in those days, frequently broke down in front of our house. Apart from the loss of compression due to a faulty engine in some cases, many failures were due to a shortage of petrol, or gasoline as it was called. In the latter case, the driver allowed his vehicle to free-wheel backwards to the bottom of the hill where he (I knew of no woman driver in those days) would turn the vehicle round and climb the hill in the reverse gear, thus facilitating the flow of the remaining drops of fuel to the engine.

The occasional visitor who stayed overnight at our house had always expressed surprise that our family was able to endure so calmly the traffic noises due to the vibration of old cars and overladen lorries labouring in their lowest gear to ascend the steep hill. In addition, there were those drivers who felt duty bound to signal their approach to the slightest of bends in the road by nervously sounding their horns over and over. That only helped to compound the issues. Strangely enough, our family had suffered no inconvenience to my knowledge – we were well-accustomed to it all.

Quite a number of accidents occurred at that corner, and my account of the various incidents so far has not touched upon the numerous events that took place relating to the traffic moving in the opposite direction.

Looking back, I firmly believe that the height of the hibiscus hedge along our front garden, and along those of our neighbours, with their prolific foliage, had created the blind corner that it was. A much lower hedge, or none at all, may have averted, or at least minimised, the numerous flights of cyclists and motor vehicles that left the bend at various tangents in their descent to crash along the embankment on the opposite side of the road.

18

Began Work in Machine Shop: Oil Company

On my father's arrival home one Saturday afternoon in October 1926, he immediately called out:

'Jacob! Jacob! Where are you?'

'I'm out here, Pa, in the garden.'

'Come . . . a minute, I have good news for you.'

Sensing the excitement in his voice, I immediately replied, 'Coming Pa,' stopped what I was doing and raced towards him at the entrance to the kitchen.

'Hello, Pa, where are they?' I asked, casually lowering my gaze and glancing around on the floor, smiling expectantly.

'What are you looking for, son?' he enquired, half smiling in return.

'The shoes you bought for me.'

'Oh no, son; I couldn't afford to buy them today. But the good news I have for you is worth much more than any shoes money can buy . . . and I'll still buy the shoes for you.'

'All right, Pa, well, what is the good news?' I enquired slightly disenchanted.

Thus, in October 1926, my long-awaited opportunity had arrived.

'Well, Jacob, at last I've got you a job. A good job, the type we were waiting for. It's a job in the machine shop,' said my father.

I was so elated that in my rush to embrace him, he was put slightly off balance. I thanked him again and again and told him that the shoes could now be purchased from my pay.

Nearly all that weekend I asked about the work in the machine shop. He explained as best he could and briefed on the various safeguards, as I was scheduled to begin work the ensuing week.

During the period from about thirteen to sixteen, I indulged in a great deal of pastimes, foremost among them being cricket, swimming, rowing and athletics as a whole. At fourteen I had attained the school-leaving age.

The old village school by the railway viaduct had taken on a more friendly atmosphere and all the good wishes and pleasantries that were observed on such occasions brought home to me the reality and the significance of the end of an epoch, studded with apprehensions and mis-givings, work and play, laughter and tears, music and song – a unique world of learning – gone forever.

I realised then, that some of the relationships will have been destined to last a lifetime. Many of the experiences gained during the period of schooling (five to fourteen) will remain ill-defined, but nevertheless will have played, and will continue to play, an important part in the fertilisation of my creativity.

Without really knowing the significance of a better education, I was thankful to my father for having kept me on at school as long as he did, for many children had long left, since compulsory education was not in force at that time as far as I knew.

At the moment of farewell, the various episodes as I saw them were compounded. Filled with emotions, I felt that I was just beginning to understand, and so appreciate, the importance of the various subjects I was taught.

On my departure, I glanced back at the school for a

moment, then once again, as I walked away with an inexplicable reluctance. I wanted to be alone for a moment, and so I fell back behind the crowd, then glancing sideways at the school in the distance, I saw at that moment a fleeting picture of my entire school life.

On retiring to bed that night, an endless ribbon of events moved slowly across my vision, unfolding evocative scenes, gladdening the heart in one instance and saddening it in another, with thoughts of my deceased mother and my Aunt Nenen. But, above all, thoughts of the occasion of my mother's death disturbed me most of all. I never really understood the circumstances and there was no one willing to talk about the matter, the great barrier being that in those days, children were not spoken with on such matters.

Further along the endless ribbon of reflections, on the skyline, the silhouette of Gupta's mammoth black bull appeared, towering over our docile little Isabelle. Still awake in the dark, thoughts of my parents filled my heart. Their role was a matter of teamwork.

I missed my mother very much . . . much more than I ever did, but I consoled myself with a determination to help my father in teamwork as my mother did, as soon as I got a job with the Oil Company. Such had been the working of my mind.

My father was determined that I should be a machinist or tradesman of some kind. Thus he was continually in search of a suitable employment for me. Meanwhile, he arranged for me to continue my education and so was engaged at my old village school as a part-time monitor for the time being.

In this elevated position I saw myself as both teacher and pupil and seemed to enjoy the status. The reason for this was due to the fact that I was not cut off from the ways of a senior pupil, and at the same time I had increased access to the means of improving my education.

In October 1926, I was fifteen and a half, and thus my long-awaited opportunity had arrived. I became one of the Oil Company's latest recruits. My father's patience and untiring efforts had been rewarded. I was assigned to what appeared to me then, a very large machine shop and began work on the 26th day of that month, at the rate of three cents per hour, one hundred cents being equal to a pound sterling at that time.

My parents had known the foreman for quite a few years, and he had frequently purchased bread and fried fish from my mother. Indeed it was due to the foreman's influence that my father was able to obtain this well-sought-after employment for me.

Mr Rolando, the foreman, middle-aged, slightly built, carried his tall figure with such sprightliness and effusion of energy as even the most intrepid of workers found his presence unsettling. He was a man of dark-brown complexion with a natural air of prudence and authority. His brown eyes, constantly darting, kept unflinching surveillance over everything and everybody. With cocked ears, Mr Rolando detected any irregularity in the rhythmic drone of the various belt-driven lathes and milling machines, pipe threading and bending machines, compressors and forges, and a host of other mechanical equipment.

My duties during the first few weeks were those of a general shop boy – sweeping up and rubbing down, and washing down the floors and benches, not to mention the running of numerous errands. This was an entirely new world to me, fascinating, bewildering and most absorbing. It seemed to be a place for grown-ups only, busying themselves in changing the shape and appearance of one thing into another. In my view at the time, metal rods were cut into bits and made into nuts and bolts; and the dirty outer skin of a metallic object would be peeled off, leaving a clean, nice and shiny surface.

The size of the machine shop seemed to be about 90 feet wide by 120 feet long. The main entrance at a gable end was fitted with a mechanically operated sliding door, and overhead pulleys and trolleys were in operation everywhere.

At the opposite end of the building a small section was partitioned off for welding purposes, and nearby stood a disconcerting array of menacingly grotesque objects. I learned afterwards that they were anvils and were an essential contrivance for the work of the blacksmith. Of course, there were several blacksmiths, and when they were at work red and white sparks streaked about at random in the compartment as a result of heavy hammer blows upon the molten mass of metal on their anvils.

Shaping the molten mass by timely hammer blows upon the anvil was usually accompanied by some display of skill by the blacksmith as a percussionist. The tuneful syncopated rhythm produced often carried with it a reminder that Trinidad was the land of the calypso.

In this dramatic display, the welders were not to be outdone. They seemed to have a peculiar form of fireworks all of their own, casting on their panels gruesome shadows symbolic of hooded phantoms with blazing strike weapon, emitting an alarming hissing sound and an irritating pungency that frequently watered the eye and clogged the nasal passages.

All those things I saw as an exciting world, full of adventure, and great opportunities for learning. I was very excited and very proud of my job, which I performed with great enthusiasm.

I continued to make satisfactory progress at work, and after six months I received a rise in pay. My family was musical but no one had been in a position to purchase a musical instrument. I rather liked the sound of the clarinet and I fancied myself to be the owner of such an instrument. After such consideration, I sent off a COD order for an instrument by post to London and began saving desperately for the cost on its arrival. News about the formation of a village band 'went on the air' and long before my clarinet arrived, there were already three prospective members with their instruments – quatro, bass and banjo.

19

The Corridor Incident

Meanwhile my progress at work continued to receive notable recognition, and it was rumoured that I would be promoted to an apprentice turner. In those days a lathe was regarded as one of the most prestigious machines in the workshop. Hence I was full of excitement and anxiously looked forward to the occasion.

Early one Monday morning before work commenced, I received a message instructing me to call on the chief mechanist. He was also deputy foreman.

'Good morning, sir; I was told to report to you, sir,' I said politely.

'Oh yes, Jacob, that's right. How would you like to operate a machine like this, eh?' he asked.

'Oh . . . I'd like to, sir; but I'd rather start with a little one and learn more about the big one as I go along,' I replied casting a glance over his huge machine – the largest lathe in the shop.

'Well, you're being given the opportunity to do just that. Your promotion begins today. You are to spend this week with me, at my machine, and next week you'll be put on your own lathe, . . . that little one over there,' said the foreman, pointing in the direction.

'How would you like that?' he added.

'Oh, I'd like that very much,' I responded briskly, smiling with excitement.

'I'll be responsible for your progress, you know, Jacob; I'm sure you won't let me down.'

'Oh no, sir, I won't, I'm sure.' After a brief moment, I said, 'Thank you very much, sir.'

I thanked him because I felt that as leading machinist, the final decision might well have been his.

In due course I settled down to my new assignment and occasionally rendered assistance to the chief machinist. It may have been his way of assessing my progress. Apart from work on the machine, I frequently ran inter-departmental errands.

Maintenance work in the refineries was of paramount importance and it is often required to carry out extremely urgent structural and mechanical repairs to equipment or machinery damaged by an explosion, fire or by some other means. The following is a brief account of a particular occurrence.

There was a terrific explosion in one of the high-pressure furnaces in the oil refinery one morning. The tube head blew off and blasted its way at high speed through adjacent structures leaving a train of blazing fire in its wake.

The charged atmosphere was immediately heightened by the wailing alarm signals at the refinery, followed by fire-fighting machines with their elaborate equipment, and the ambulance, all making themselves heard as distinctly as possible. Within moments a list of priorities was rushed to the machine shop.

'Jacob, Jacob!' hailed the foreman.

A damaged section of machinery was hurriedly brought for urgent repairs by the manager of the plant in question. He and a few high officials were discussing the implications when I was called.

'Yes sir,' I answered the call of the foreman.

'Dash over to the garage, quickly, and find the foreman

133

and tell him to let me have right away, the special double-ended spanner he borrowed from me yesterday. Hurry lad, hurry!' said the shop foreman, expressing great urgency.

The garage was connected to the machine shop by a corridor six feet wide by forty feet long, flanked on both sides by offices opening onto it.

In hasty pursuit of the spanner, I darted off through unhindered passages in the machine shop and on to the corridor which led to the garage.

Mr Winnicot, the assistant manager of the production plant for which the emergency repair was being done, was in the process of making his exit from the machine shop superintendent's office into the said corridor. Within a split second, I instinctively veered away from colliding with Mr Winnicot but not without giving him an embarrassing shock. With his reputation as an outstanding football player, he also, took spontaneous evasive action as he revenged on me with a demoralizing kick on my buttocks.

Momentarily jolted off the floor and propelled out of balance, stumbling and staggering, I regained my composure in time to discharge my errand successfully.

It was rather ironic that I should have been such an ardent follower of Mr Winnicot for his wizardry at both football and rugby on the playing field. He was exceptionally brilliant and I frequently went to see him play at several matches, even from behind fencing. Tall and handsome he carried his well-built frame with an attractive elegance. Black hair and deep blue eyes were not a common combination for a white man in those days, as far as I can recall. No one had witnessed the corridor incident.

Some moments later, I reflected upon the whole affair: during the fleeting moments that I was assailed in the corridor, from the moment of the impact of the heavy boot upon my person to the moment I regained 'consciousness' so to speak, I was not aware of anything around me, and the experience was very similar to the unconscious state I suffered on the occasion of my scooter accident when I was thirteen. In this case, however, it was as though I were completely protected and sheltered in the manner of the phenomenon of synonymity with Jacob as described in the narrative. And here too I had sensed the atmosphere of the hallowing tranquillity I had always experienced in such instances, and had attached to it the presence of Lamont since early childhood. Much later on I concluded that the source was spiritual and I am of that conviction even at this moment of writing.

There were instances, too, in which, even as a little boy, when confronted with certain difficulties, problems of forebodings from time to time, I frequently sensed a notion of heightened confidence and well-being. And what was more, I seemed to have been able to precipitate the process in the case of desperation. This phenomenon had always been, and is still, very difficult to appreciate. I believe that it is a protective device in the make-up of all human beings. With regard to 'Lamont', the perception is rather more subtle than the synonymity phenomenon with Jacob, and appears to operate in situations of dire straits, leaving in its wake an atmosphere of hope and cheerfulness, and a spirit of animation.

I have long conceded my ignorance on such matters and have accepted them as a blessing. They may well constitute to some measure some of the characteristics of the entire human race. I regard this phenomenon, personally, as an automatic response to the deepest impulse of the human soul.

The corridor assault marked the end of my admiration for Mr Winnicot. I had heard awful remarks about his special dislike for black people but I'd not seen any sign of it, and I disbelieved everything I'd heard so far. Obviously, evidence had come to light. Even so, he might not have been as bad as all that had been said of him, for my case could have been far worse for me. A member of the staff was always right and, had I been accused of racing along the corridor and had caused them a terrible fright, my position would have been rather insecure despite the booting I had had.

I was wrong to run at speed along the passage but I didn't think I deserved that form of punishment. I was deeply hurt emotionally but I told no one about the incident. I wanted to keep my job. I had just turned sixteen.

20

Transferred to Engineering Drawing Office

About four weeks later, a new scheme was introduced by the Firm whereby each apprentice in the machine shop would have to spend one year in the engineering drawing office in order to enable him to read and understand the details specified on the blue-print. By this time there were about five apprentices in the machine shop, and selection had to be decided by a written test on English composition, arithmetic and general knowledge.

The following day I was summoned to the superintendent's office. It was my first visit to his office.

Upon entering he said, 'Sit down, Jacob,' as he directed me to the chair in front of the desk at which he was seated. 'Well,' he said, sitting back leisurely in his chair. 'I see you've gained top marks in each paper; you've therefore earned the merit to be the first candidate to be transferred from the machine shop to the drawing office on the Apprenticeship Scheme. How do you feel about it?' he asked.

'I'm very pleased about it, sir;' I would like that very much,' I replied with a restrained smile.

It was only then that I really took notice of another white gentleman seated next to him. I was now more relaxed.

'I suppose you know all about the Apprenticeship Scheme,' said the chief draughtsman to whose department I was going to be transferred.

'I have an idea, sir,' I replied.

'Good, but I think I'd better explain anyway . . . you'll be transferred to the drawing office as from next Monday and will continue your employment there, in my department, for one year after which period you'll return to the machine shop to complete your apprenticeship. Do you follow?'

'Yes sir.'

'Well, is there any question you'd like to ask?' intervened the machine shop superintendent. I hesitated for a moment, then replied, 'Oh, yes sir; what clothes should I wear, sir?'

'Oh, that's a point . . . just ordinary; just as though you were going to school – not to the machine shop.'

'Thank you, sir,' I said once again.

Both men looked at each other and smiled as they gathered up their files on the desk. At that point I felt qualified for the post by virtue of the result of the Test Paper. I understood later that assessment of my character, appearance, general behaviour and the machine shop's report on my progress were all crucial factors.

During a quiet re-appraisal of the effects issuing from the disgrace of being kicked, in the privacy of my bedroom during the following night I realized how entrenched I was in the habit of relating major events in the course of my life to the time period of certain occurrences recorded in the Holy Bible. I firmly believed then, and I believe at the time of writing, that one's profound belief in one's ability to accomplish a desired end, with due resolve, would be achieved eventually, even though the mode and manner may be somewhat stressful.

That night I wept bitterly as horrible thoughts raced through my head, criss-crossing and exploding in collision in my brain. I reeled and turned and twisted with anguish in my bed, and tossed to the foot of the bed, ending on the floor with tear-soaked handkerchiefs that had long served their usefulness. No one knew of my secret heartaches. My mother would have known, but she was dead. She died nearly five years ago in defending the cause of the family, the details of which had never been fully clarified.

It was not until I was fifteen that I became better informed of what might have been the case, as described earlier in this narrative. Indeed, those were the days when even youths who were regarded as being respectable and discreet were still kept in check with regard to free and open conversation with the adult community of the village.

In recovering from the greatest impact of the shock and regaining control of myself, I recounted some of the notable biblical recordings. Still wide awake in the dead of night, I recalled that in the creation of the world the seventh day was of special significance, and that human behaviour was responsible for an incident which lasted for a duration of forty days and forty nights. And of course, in our times – much nearer so – we have the most vivid reminders of the Resurrection which occurred on the third day.

Of those notable events, I considered the period of three days was the shortest; thus I decided to put an end to my torment on the third day following my humiliation in the corridor.

I had given the matter considerable thought and finally decided to take some positive action to avenge my hurt and so lift myself out of the doldrums, and regain my pride. I reflected the occasion during which it was alleged that one of my uncles became 'invisible' by some special invocation, when he was pursued by a Police Inspector for an alleged offence. From that moment his reputation as a man of 'Powerful Prayers' rose to great heights by those who had witnessed the incident, and he was considered to be a man with whom one should not tamper lest he should put a curse upon the offender.

It was hardly six months prior to the corridor incident that this very uncle had taken me into his confidence and had explained to me the purpose of some of those 'Powerful prayers'. Indeed they were handed down from past generations, and I was a privileged recipient of some remnants. As a result, I felt myself fully capable of avenging Mr Winnicot for having kicked me so viciously.

'Yes, I could do that and no one would know,' I said to myself.

'Oh no,' a familiar voice interrupted my line of thought.

'What have you in mind anyway?' the questioner asked.

It was Lamont in the role of counsellor.

'Well, I had thought of having his left leg broken in an accident while playing a football match, painlessly of course,' I added quickly.

'What good will you derive from that?'

'Some satisfaction I suppose . . . the satisfaction of making him realize that he committed a foul deed with that same leg and he may repent for the good of his soul. In that way, I feel that I would be doing him a favour as well as myself,' I remarked.

'And suppose he didn't repent?' said Lamont.

'Well, then he could be made to lose the leg just as many black people in Africa had lost their limbs and even their wives at the hands of invading white people in various parts of Africa.'

Such was the trend of my thoughts at that particular moment.

Just as Lamont was becoming sympathetic towards me, a becalming atmosphere pervaded my bedroom, and set me pondering the question: 'How would that help me to achieve my purpose in this life?'

I knew at once that it was the response of my own irrepressible soul. Forthwith, I dismissed the idea of putting a curse upon Mr Winnicot, and prayed for his forgiveness. I suppose that I was nearly sixteen. My thoughts and general behaviour were in keeping with my upbringing and as such, my conclusion was inevitable.

Being thus satisfied, I settled down with a firm determination to work hard, and carefully, always bearing in mind that anything I undertake to do should be done to the best of my ability, in accordance with my father's principle. This was a great relief for the thought of a curse made me shudder with fear.

A few days prior to the date on which it had been arranged for me to return to the machine shop, the chief draughtsman called me into his office. My heart leaped into my throat and lingered there, beating aloud, I thought. I knocked on the door.

'Come in . . . sit down,' he said, glancing at a letter on the desk at which he was seated. Looking up at me with a welcome smile, he said, 'Well, your file has just been returned from the machine shop superintendent with his reply to my request. It has been agreed that you should remain here, in the drawing office on a permanent basis. Therefore you'll not be going back to the machine shop. I presumed that you would prefer that. How do you feel about it?' he remarked, and sat back leisurely, awaiting my response.

'Oh yes, sir, I prefer to stay here . . . very much, thank you. . . .'

I do not recall the exact sequence of events following that momentous occasion, but the manner of his announcement cannot be forgotten. My heart had returned to its normal place but I was left walking on air for several days, in a state of sublime animation.

During the ensuing weeks of composure, I looked at several advertisements and decided to enrol for a comprehensive course on draughtsmanship – Engineering, Drawing and Design, from a correspondence college in England. In due course, my first set of lessons arrived by post together with books on field work. Thus, I was set on the right road, and on a sound footing. The opportunity for a native black employee to acquire practical experience in the layout of plants and in topographical surveying had not been known hitherto.

21

Special Interest in Birds

My fascination for birds had begun before I was four years of age. Their plumage, their song, their flight through the air, their walk or hop, and indeed their general behaviour, including the building of their nests and care of their young, had always held my interest. The first to have caught my attention was the humming-bird as it flew along the hibiscus hedge at the front of our yard, dipping its long beak into each of the radiant flowers in succession. Everything about this little bird seemed so marvellous, and its greatest appeal to me as a child was at the moment during which it remained hovering close to the flower on its approach. I often whispered to it and told it how beautiful it was with its tail nicely fanned out. I was never able to distinguish any change of action of its wings due to the rapidity of movement.

The pretty little bird was able to fly forwards or backwards, and dart away at an astonishing speed. Surprisingly, too, one of the traits of the humming-bird was the molesting of much larger birds, the owl and the huge corbeau being no exception.

There were many other birds which held my interest too, but in quite a different way. That which attracted my attention most of all was the cravat, as it was called in our village. I suppose the beautiful bird was known throughout the island for its lovely song as well as its manner and good looks. I have not had the opportunity to learn about our national livestock during my school days; I refer, therefore, mainly to those animals and birds with which I had firm knowledge or personal dealings.

In my youth, I saw black birds, green birds, and scarlet or red birds fly past in formation high up in the sky, but no one in our village seemed to know what type of birds they were, or from whence they came, or to where they were going. Very much later on, I learned that the flock of red birds I had seen may have been the scarlet ibis, regarded as one of our national birds.

The cravat, my favourite bird, was noted for its beautiful song while in flight as well as on its perch, generally on tall trees. It is easily distinguished in flight by its undulation, sometimes dipping quite suddenly and steeply in its speedy passage through the air. The plumage of the male was particularly beautiful with colours of black, navy blue, light yellow and gold, speckled with green around the neck. The female, on the other hand, was of a grey-yellow. These birds were somewhat difficult to catch, but were easily tamed and survived very well in captivity.

At thirteen or thereabout, I spent a great deal of my spare time rowing, fishing and sea bathing at Campeche Bay. Spinning tops, bird catching, kite-flying and playing cricket – all such things had received much of my attention. It was during that period, too, that my responsibility at home had increased considerably. Looking back, I wondered how on earth I managed it all.

My actual bird-catching experience began with parakeets. They were a menace to our corn crop. They were sturdy birds with sparkling green and yellow plumage. They had a lusty appetite, and were very vicious when caught. But trapping them was the only effective means of safeguarding our corn crop at that time. Their noisy and bad-tempered manner did not appeal to me and therefore I did not keep the parakeet in my possession for any length of time.

The ground dove and the mountain dove were not such a menace to our crops although they sometimes attacked the newly planted seed. They were trapped mainly for the table, and I must say that as a child I rather relished the art of catching them with the minimum of contraption. They were easy prey, however, and did not offer much of a challenge.

My favourite, on the other hand, had offered much more of a challenge. I revert to the cravat. They were high-flying birds that fed on a particular parasite in the form of a weed known in my childhood days as 'varge', frequently found on the tallest trees. There were times, of course, when a prolific bunch of varge was discovered on a relatively shorter tree in an out of-the-way place, thus offering the greatest opportunity for their entrapment. They were cunning birds and were not easily caught. The discovery of a good feeding place was the primary requirement in the attempt to catch them. With easy access to the bunch of parasite, with ripened seeds, two or three thin rods coated with laglee – a sticky substance obtained from the sap of certain plants – often sufficed in this particular venture. The coated sticks were then placed among the stems and branches of the varge as additional perches. By deception, the bird was stuck fast, unknowingly, until it attempted to fly away. Often my colleagues and I would have concealed ourselves at the foot of the tree and imitated the song of the bird and so lured them to their feeding place.

The other method of catching the cravat was by placing a similar bird, already tamed, in a cage next to the varge on the tree. With a trap-cage attached, the song of the tame bird would lure those in the wild to the feeding place,

145

and eventually into the trap-cage with the intention of making a closer acquaintanceship. When the trap-door flies there would be a quick flutter, often overlooked by the fervour of the new friendship.

The newly-caught bird had to be specially attended for a period of a week or two depending upon the temperament and intelligence of the particular bird. The new bird was best served being placed in a comparatively large cage, sometimes with a tame bird as companion, in this way the new bird would copy its mate, and the difficulty in adapting to its new diet would have been averted or minimised and, likewise, the fatality due to the odd hunger strike!

The new diet in those days consisted of banana, their favourite being 'Grand Michel' or 'Governor Fig' (fig was the common name for the banana). The method of enticing the bird to its new diet consisted in holding its legs securely between thumb and fingers and allowing free movement of the wings. With the other hand, a partly peeled banana was brought quickly to the beak of the bird. In some form of defence, the banana was attacked by a peck or two. The palatable beak full of juicy banana was inevitably swallowed, and soon appreciated. The purpose was invariably served in that manner.

The cravat, a high-flyer as I knew it, was a sophisticated bird. Its song would be heard far away in the distance, piercing the atmosphere, and engendering a feeling of tranquillity. A distinct melancholy somehow prevailed, fleetingly animating the mind with some form of inspiration and hope for the future. Such were my personal emotions and experience in respect of the cravat.

By far the most spectacular method of trapping birds during the period of my youth was the employment of the basket trap. The basket would be made of bamboo in the shape of a 'basket' as its name implies, preferably in the

146

shape of a rectangle. This form of trap was more suitable for the ground doves, mountain doves and wild pigeons. These birds were not the menace to our corn crop as presented by the flocks of parakeets, but they were a delicacy on the table. In all these matters, however, my principal concern was to learn the art of catching them. With the basket trap several birds were often caught in one fell swoop, and there would be quite a flutter, for a brief moment.

Another form of trap was called the Flying Trap. In this case a natural feeding ground in the woods was selected and a clearance of about four square yards was made. The central portion would be staked out, dividing the whole into two separate parts, except for a passage of about twelve inches in the middle. The stakes were driven firmly into the ground to a height of about ten inches and spaced about one inch apart. The king posts, one at each end of the twelve-inch passage, were slightly taller than the rest. When staked out, the area seemed like a miniature tennis court with a passage in the middle. Bird seed or ground corn, oats and the like, were scattered in each 'court'. A crosspiece was placed between the king posts at a height of about two inches, so that a bird in its leisurely walk from one side to the other would hop upon the crossbar. An appropriate mechanism would trigger off the flying trap as the weight of the bird depressed the crosspiece, and dislodged its support. A suitable young tree, stripped of its branches and leaves, at a height of about six feet would be bent over in an arc with a fine cord attached to the stalk and well secured. A suitable lasso would be placed over the crosspiece to overlap a section of each 'court'. In hopping upon the crosspiece, the bird's leg or legs hardly escaped the lasso.

A similar contraption was applied to trap the mongoose which was the greatest menace to our chickens. In this case a hole would be dug in the ground at a depth of six inches and at an angle of forty-five degrees, with a bait consisting of fish. The arched stalk of the tree – flying stick – with the lasso placed at the periphery of the entrance to the hole, would be set to fly when the animal would have made its bid for the rotting fish. All this may sound rather gruesome but it was rewarding to be rid of an animal which frequently deprived us of some of our valuable feathered livestock.

22

Dreams and Nightmares

In retrospect, I seemed to have an aptitude for many types of games and sporting activities. As a child, and in my early teens I was always engaged in one field or another, and may have been over-active or over-sensitive at times, especially between the ages of twelve and fifteen.

I recall having had frequent nightmares during that period, and they all seemed related to the activities in which I had been currently involved. They occurred at intervals of about three weeks or less at times. As strange as they were, and often gruesome, I had never been in a state of real panic for I had acquired the habit of awakening myself at the crucial moment. The nightmares had always taken the form of a chase, and it was I who was being chased every time, by one of the most venomous of creatures to boot – a deadly snake. Such nightmares may have been due to the numerous tales I had heard from time to time, but it was rather strange that the reaction should have been delayed until the period of puberty.

There were times, however, when they were a direct result of what had actually transpired a day or so before. For example, during the school holiday I was among a group of boys. We must have been about ten years old, and all in impish mood on our way to the beach, a short distance away. Brian, one of the boys, had a bright idea and spoke out. 'I say everyone stop! Stop it! Let us ambush some black jack Spaniards,' (vicious black wasps) suggested Brian, a forward type of boy. 'Yes, yes why don't we?' was the response. There was a unanimous agreement, only a slight detour was necessary, and there was the target to be attacked – a huge nest of angry wasps, about thirty feet up in a tree.

We furtively gathered our missiles – stones, bits of wood, old or even ripe fruit – anything that would give the nest a good jolt. And that we did effectively. But the wasps were fully prepared for us. En masse, they left their nest instantly and pursued us with such obstinacy as rendered all our evasive actions utterly futile. Not one of us had escaped the virulence of their wrath. Some time later, a similar incident occurred in the form of a nightmare, but then I had the presence of mind (in the nightmare) to dive into a swift flowing river which was rather handy. That was effectively evasive, but the thought of a cataract awaiting me downstream was too terrifying to contemplate. Thus, I tossed and tossed myself in bed, and awakened myself to avert what would have been a greater catastrophe – had it been real.

There were several instances in which a reptile of one kind or another was involved. And these too were related to some personal experience. Let me refer to my encounter with a grass snake. First of all, one of my younger brothers had come face to face with this particular snake when he was about six. He went to fetch a bucket of water from the stand-pipe just across the road facing our house. It was a hot sunny afternoon and a grass snake – wiry in nature – may have been rather thirsty, for there it was, at the base of the stand pipe near the little pool of water due to a dripping tap, or the overflow from a bucket. Thus confronted, my brother called out to me for help while he and the snake kept an eye on each other, each being afraid to make the first move.

This type of snake was believed to be non-poisonous but none was ever quite certain about such things, except in the case of those well-known to be venomous due to the effects of their attacks on hunters and their dogs. I was nearly thirteen and had the responsibility of looking after the affairs of the home while my father was away at work. In response to my brother's call I hurried over across the road, armed with cutlass and stick, fully prepared to do battle in defence of my younger brother. As soon as I arrived at the spot, this wiry creature with beady eyes sunken into a slightly flattened tiny head, suddenly contracted its coil and emitted a series of disquieting hisses. I was completely taken aback, for I had never imagined so small a head would contain a mouth so frightfully large with a white hollowness which extended far beyond my imagination.

As children, we were told about deadly snakes that formed themselves into a coil, like a spring, and when released, sail through the air at speed and wrap themselves around their victims, to squeeze the life out of them. And again, the most vicious type of all, anchors itself to the ground, or to a tree stump and flicks out at you and gets back in place ready to strike again, and it never misses.

With all these abominable thoughts racing through my mind, the threatening snake, seemingly afraid to lower its guard, stood its ground, waiting for me to take the initiative. Well, well . . . I thought to myself, if this is to be a pitched battle, my three-foot-long stick would be far too short for this horrible creature. The cutlass was even shorter. Moreover I'd ruled out the cutlass at the very moment I saw the snake open its mouth, because it was said that there was nothing more disastrous than a snake's head hanging on to your flesh in its final act of defence.

Thus I darted back home across the road, and was back

in no time, with a long bamboo pole. Standing well clear with my brother also out of the way, I took aim and charged in such a way that the snake would have found it impossible to slither up the pole to attack me. That cumbersome charge was all bravado but it was more than the frightened creature was able to endure. Like a flash of light, it disappeared in the bushes nearby. My brother was relieved and so was I. Moments later, he brought in the bucket full of water, smiling all over his face. I did not touch upon the subject. I did not ask him what he was smiling about either.

And so, accounting my nightmares, they often began in a field somewhere in the form of an adventurous enterprise. Another typical example is in the form of my being chased by the most venomous of all snakes. I ran as fast as I could but never seemed to increase my lead. In fact, the snake always seemed to be gaining on me. At that moment I took to the air like a mighty big bird, and to my astonishment the viper sprouted wings and took off in my pursuit, gradually gaining on me but not quite catching up. At a very young age, I had observed many birds in flight and the most impressive, if not the fastest, seemed to have been the pelican or the corbeau, in its descent from a great height.

And so in the nightmare, I would ride the warm air and circle my way up to a very great height. But the snake would still be there, following me very closely. Suddenly, I took a steep dive heading for the waters where I learned to swim, in the surroundings with which I was most familiar. My steep dive took me to a great depth in the sea. Breaking off sharply, I rose to the surface and took to the air again without a moment's hesitation, leaving the viper floundering and sinking in the deep with its sprawling water-sodden wings. The snakes in all my nightmares had never been able to overcome this stage of their pursuit.

152

And, it was just as well they'd found it impossible, I thought.

*   *   *

Of all the dreams and nightmares I have experienced, I regard the following as being most moving and the most complex. I found it profoundly absorbing . . . full of foreboding and yet exquisitely delightful in parts. It occurred when I was about twenty and was physically indisposed for a few weeks, seemingly unable to cope with the various issues under my charge.

During my predicament in the dream I felt that I was being consumed and confounded by some regressive forces under the influence of a strangely potent anaesthetic, and despite my benumbment I'd sensed at intervals a gradual transformation. My greatest puzzlement was the seemingly dual state of existence, sometimes in juxtaposition and on other occasions in two tiers, somewhere in the remote past. There were repetitions of the nightmare. At first I dispelled the whole affair as fantasy then gradually I began to see it as a special phenomenon, implicitly warning against overtaxing my nervous system. I believed then, that all human beings had such a mechanism.

My recollections of events in this particular case started at the very beginning of my awareness. I must have been an orphan. At about three years of age I found myself wandering about a field, wading through thick grass and shrubbery in a sad state of exhaustion. I knew not where I was. I saw no one and did not recall knowing anyone. My only recollection was that I was called Jacob. I may have fainted or fallen asleep from exhaustion. On awakening I found myself being nursed to recovery by a family of five in a spacious bedroom. I recalled then that at the last moments in the prairie I had caught a glimpse of a large white house in the distance through the foliage of surrounding trees. And now I was being nurtured in that very house.

I recalled quite clearly that I was not able to give any experience about my whereabouts, and extensive enquiries in the vicinity had proved futile. I was therefore adopted by Mr and Mrs Martello. They were the most prominent farmer/landlords in the district to all accounts. Thus, I appeared to have been well-placed. There were three daughters in the family, the youngest of which was about six years old. Being the only boy in the household considerable fuss was made of me and I felt secure as an integral party of the family. But the novelty of having a baby boy in the family was short-lived as I grew older. There was no loss of love and affection but I knew that without a good knowledge of farming I may be confined to no more than the menial tasks . . . Such was my reasoning so far in my dream.

By some remarkable coincidence these nightmares were repeated in parts or extended with some deviations; as a result the complete picture would best be portrayed by the compilation of the relevant episodes in chronological order. With that in view I shall continue to explain what I believe to be one of the most unsettling phenomena I've hitherto encountered.

To continue my account of the strange dream in question, I refer back to the point (in the dream) at which I saw no future worthwhile for me: Life at home in the farmhouse had begun to appear slightly strained despite the usual love and affection, but I was growing up and had begun to understand the various forces at play in the community. I soon learnt to adapt to the wiles and volatility so blatantly audible and overtly expressed. For instance, Mr Martello was reputed to be a mean man with a terrible temper. Very tall and with very broad thick shoulders. He was versed in the habit of not listening to anyone, for he was deaf. In addition to that, he was in the habit of pushing his way past everyone in a corridor, passageway or in the market place, shouldering them off-balance and behaved as though nothing had ever occurred, except for a broad grin on rare occasions. He was a very important man in the community, very impatient and totally destitute of any form of refinement.

Mrs Martello was in many ways an endearing foster-mother but her merits were best appreciated from a little way off. She was a very large woman who, like her husband was a 'juggernaut' determined not to be outdone by her husband and her most important instrument for the purpose was her vitriolic tongue. As I grew older I was assigned to more and more menial tasks but I was put to some useful work on the plantation as well. I had never been denied any of the basic requirements.

I must have spent quite a long time with my foster-parents working on the farm for at fourteen, I had learnt much about the management and workings of the estate. I had always been shown love and affection by the entire family but now I seemed to have grown much closer to their hearts than ever. Despite it all I had a compelling urge to widen my horizon and had begun to resign myself to that idea.

Time passed quickly, I was seventeen and decided to inform my foster-parents. I expressed my thanks and gratitude for all they did for me. They both had an idea that I would soon be moving on and wished me well.

On leaving my foster-parents' estate I turned right at the winding road which ran along the front of the property. Within forty-five minutes I entered a very attractive town. I was very impressed with it and was fortunate to obtain employment there within a week. It was a small Engineering Firm with pleasant staff and surroundings. I decided to pursue a career, and three years later on the occasion of my annual holiday (in the dream) I encountered an incident in my 'odyssey' which had an overwhelming effect upon me, and may have been a turning point in my life in some way or other.

I've always had a fascination for mountains and this is reflected prominently. In the dreams I was in the habit of going off alone high up in the foothills, and now there was an irresistible urge to visit those heights once more as though in response to an urgent call. I had had exclusive use of a small cabin perched high up on a sheltered plateau and took immediate steps to reserve it once again. On the day in question, I set off early and bright of spirit to keep at bay the occasional anxious moments.

My early trek deep into the forest seemed familiar and as endless as on previous occasions. The atmosphere, however, now seemed weird and gloomy, overshadowed by a kind of living darkness, pierced here and there by shafts of sunlight puncturing the canopy of clustered leaves and branches of the dome. At length my first rugged ascent had begun, up and up to a plateau; then to another and finally up to the soothing serenity of the cabin. Despite my arduous ascent I recovered very quickly and reviewed the familiar features of the surroundings.

I had planned to spend four weeks in those glorious heights, mainly relaxing and meditating. I viewed the world from a different angle and felt at times to be at one with nature. And now, on the penultimate day of my holiday, there were speculative signs of gloom. The peculiar glow of the sun and its sudden disappearance behind heavy dark grey clouds were forebodings of an unusual kind; I thus completed packing for my departure the following day and retired to the safety of the cabin in readiness for any eventuality during those last hours of my holiday. I soon became aware of an approaching storm, gathering pace. With windows, shutters and door secured, reliable lighted lantern on a solid little table beside my campbed, I was as cosy as ever I cared.

All creatures scurried away from the locality as the raging storm advanced and halted abruptly at a distance of about thirty yards from the cabin. The reverberations from the elements pointed a clear picture of the likely prospects outside the cabin. But inside too, an unsavoury situation had begun to emerge. The light began to flicker rapidly and a sudden infiltration of a peculiar darkness began filling up the cabin. The source of supply seemed inexhaustible and relentlessly it kept filling up the room, undulating, gyrating and seemingly regurgitating upon itself, filling the room up to overflowing.

The light had stopped flickering and was at its lowest intensity. It occurred to me then that the room may soon be destitute of oxygen and that I should get into bed immediately. And so quietly, I retired to bed. The light went out instantly. With my eyes firmly shut, I saw even more clearly, bales and bales of that depressing blackness as if from an ancient chimney stack, billowing and billowing in a hurry to fill up the cabin. Even in my dream, that was more than I'd bargained for. Already virtually breathless, I appealed for Heavenly grace and assistance to be delivered from my predicament as I'd done in the past. In less than one minute later I experienced a feeling of entombment within crumbling walls, closing me in with exquisite gentleness. Some time later I vaguely recalled being led out of the cabin and away into a blind alley, down through bewildering cataracts of the ages, and into an enormous Void where even silence seemed to echo. An unsettling state of emptiness and inaction seemed to be the state of affairs. I

157

had sensed the presence of other beings but like myself they were without form. . . . Exhausted and perplexed by the numerous events, I tossed and tossed myself to stop the nightmare. I often wondered whether the tragic loss of my mother when I was only eleven had any bearing on this particular nightmare. Fortunately, it has long ceased to recur.

23

Twisted Vengeance

Despite the close camaraderie that existed among our village folk, there were many petty acts of jealousy and rivalry that often tweaked the human spirit to an extent beyond which peaceful solutions were impracticable. And frequently, the matter spilled over at a game of cards. It took then only the slightest of arguments to develop into an explosive situation. Aided and abetted by one of the most insidious products of the industrialised sugar-cane – alcohol – a rapid breakdown of good relationship was the inevitable result.

At their various meeting places, or gambling dens, as they were sometimes called, in back gardens, or in the bushes or woods here or there, the sudden rustling of bushes often signalled the plight of the participants. A desperate hustle was often due to the weaker, or the weakest, making a hurried retreat from a fight in which he would be at the losing end.

But here again, like the cascabel, well-known for its hasty retreat from the area of disturbance, and its return to do battle, the card-player would, in like manner, return, suitably armed. In order to avoid an ambush, his opponent would be around waiting in preparation, and battle would ensue in reality. Indeed it may be a running battle lasting several hours, or it may last for several days. A stick, knife, bamboo rod, cutlass, pole or brick may be part of the general armoury of opposing groups; and victory, as far as I can remember, was never conceded or claimed, for just beneath the surface, the urge to settle old scores impatiently awaited the appropriate stimulus. Nevertheless, a particular conflict was frequently brought to a halt by the spilling of blood. Thus in brawls extending over long periods, one was able to see quite clearly, contrast in tactic and contrast in bulk and body weight of the various protagonists, and so assess their potential capabilities. Looking back later on, I was amazed at the accuracy of our judgment as youngsters.

Fortunately, such upheavals were confined to just a few individuals, and the fact that nearly everyone was related to one another meant that the whole affair was generally overlooked without any trace of suspicion by the casual visitor. There were odd occasions, it was rumoured long ago, when certain disputes were extended beyond the realm of human pacification, and intervention of the supernatural had been solicited with disastrous consequences. The following is an account which stemmed from an old grudge.

Samoo, who lived in the neighbourhood of our village, was known as a 'sleight-of-hand' gambler – a cheat – and a fighter to boot. During one of his notable visits to our village, he had boasted about his prowess as a master gambler and reminded his petty audience that on his previous visit to the village he had won the entire pay packet from three of their colleagues. This may have been Samoo's way of seeking a psychological advantage before the start of their card game, but it was taken as an affront, thus souring the atmosphere beforehand, with the effect of a pre-heated oven – set for action.

It so happened that Pinto who had volunteered to take part in the game on this occasion, had in fact lost his pay packet to Samoo on his previous participation. Pinto had suspected Samoo of cheating then, and wanted all his money back. It took a group of four men, it was said, to prevent Pinto from tearing Samoo apart.

Prior to such events, all hands met in the rum shop to prime themselves for the fray and, invariably, would be fully stocked up with reserve bottles of the beverage. Pinto had vowed not to show his hand but await his chance to avenge Samoo for the unfair loss of his entire pay packet on their previous encounter. And now the moment had arrived. Samoo, thinking that Pinto was the most vulnerable of his opponents at card games, did in fact challenge him forthwith.

'Ah Pinto, we meet again, brother. I tell you right away, you going lose all your money again today, 'cause I'm better now,' Samoo remarked mockingly with a broad grin which displayed a large mouth packed full of broad overlapping yellow teeth.

'Samoo, your biggest trouble is your mouth . . . too big and too loud. I tell you now, if you're not careful I'll fix it for you,' remarked Pinto sharply.

'All right, brother, all right. Let's settle one thing at a time. Cards first, anything could come after,' said Samoo whose remark met with urgent approval by supporters of both sides.

With frowning foreheads and cutting glances, both men shook hands, as customary, in so-called friendship, and took their respective positions at an improvised table in a clearance among the bushes.

News of the contest had only just got to Arthur and Luther. The former was a staunch supporter of Samoo, and Luther, of Pinto. Arthur and Luther were antagonistic towards each other and yet they were nearly always together. Hurrying down to the secret hideout, they argued about the possible outcome of the contest and betted against each other.

161

Both Arthur and Luther were of African descent. The former, short and agile, always prompted the latter into arguments of one form or another, with a pungent aggression.

'You know, Luther, Samoo going have it easy today, and Pinto lose bad,' Arthur remarked. It had just turned 2.00 p.m.

'What make you say so?'

'Well, you see, Samoo is a real good boxer, a wrestler and all-round fighter, and I think the whole thing going end up in a big fight.'

'I think so too, but I believe Pinto will win all-round.'

'And what makes you so sure?' asked Arthur.

'Pinto was training hard, and don't forget he can cut down any man with a hammer kick to the top of the head even when he's walking away. They ain't call him the mule for nothing, you know,' asserted Luther, as he glanced down at his shorter companion, with the certainty that Pinto was in a very revengeful mood. 'We'll soon find out, anyway,' he added.

Both Samoo and Pinto were fearless, taller than average and purposeful in their pursuits. Pinto, however, was the sturdier, of African descent, whereas Samoo of Indian. Everyone had sensed the growing atmosphere and stood on the alert, crouching or squatting from a vantage point, to view the flicking of the cards on the top of an old soap box nestled among the bushes.

On this occasion, a declared battle for supremacy once and for all, quickly spread; a battle much tougher than Samoo had ever imagined and it became obvious that after a long struggle he had begun to lose patience, and was obviously losing the game. In a desperate attempt to recover his ground, Samoo attempted one of his lightning tricks, but Pinto was on the lookout, with superb reflex, grabbed Samoo by the collar of his shirt and pulled him

162

forward. The impact of three vicious butts at close range, on Samoo's nose sent him reeling backwards with his face streaming with blood. But Samoo, the boxer, sprang to his feet and retaliated with a telling left hook to Pinto's jaw, then a right and a left to the body.

On breaking off the encounter, Pinto turned away. Believing that he was on the run, Samoo attempted to follow up the chase, and in the twinkling of an eye, his head and throat were prime targets for Pinto's devastating back kick. Samoo crumpled into a heap . . . unconscious.

Pinto, claiming the right to 'finish him off', was effectively restrained by his admirers. Momentarily they were relieved from their main concern, for Samoo, in the process of recovery, had begun to stir – he was not dead.

Within a few minutes, Samoo appeared to have fully recovered and promptly made his departure, in humiliation, leaving behind the money he had fairly won. Despite the fact that it was the general belief that Samoo had brought misfortune upon himself, there was a feeling of sympathy on his behalf.

Within a week, Samoo lay in wait for Pinto's wife, and in the ambush had badly beaten her up in revenge, in a quiet section of the road at night. In the struggle, she had sustained multiple bruises and a broken arm. Pinto immediately set out in search of Samoo but for weeks on end Samoo was nowhere to be found.

Few people in the village had heard of the incident which, as any other incident, would have died a natural death in the course of time. For Pinto, however, the dust had by no means settled, and he continued his search for Samoo's hideout. All attempts had failed, and Pinto, in desperation, decided to take what he considered to be the ultimate step. He had heard of some odd practices, and had read some odd books, and putting two and two together, he decided to take the plunge – the invocation of the dead, to seek out Samoo.

He had spent months in preparation for the occasion, and as the days went by, the more determined he became in his quest for vengeance. He carried out his research carefully, and secretly located the grave of the most notorious criminal that ever lived in the district. Resolved to invoke the spirit of that long departed criminal in pursuit of his goal, he took the necessary steps, realising the risk of great harm to himself, but had studied in detail all the precautions to be taken, and he had done so, arriving at the peak of his preparation, regretfully, one day too early.

It was a night in the week when it was alleged that the spirit of the departed should on no account be disturbed, but fearing a lack of confidence could engulf him should there be a postponement by even a day, Pinto decided to proceed with his plans being well prepared for any eventuality.

Thus, no sooner had the clock in the church tower overlooking the graveyard begun to strike the midnight hour, than Pinto began his ceremonial dance on his entry to the cemetery. Suddenly, the darkness appeared to be the darkest of all dark night he had ever seen. Uttering strange ancient words in a form of incantation handed down from his great-great-great-grandfather, he danced his way along his chosen path to the massive, over-sized grave of the once-notorious murderer. A short distance away, he came to a sudden stop and commanded the dead to rise forth.

Pinto had kept in motion constantly, uttering strange words in repetition. He issued forth another command, then another, and at this stage a weird, frightening groan emanated from the depth of the earth. There was an air of protestation in the response, and Pinto quickened his actions and resorted to the sprinkling of various substances from small bottles as he repeated his command with greater and greater emphasis.

A brisk shudder raced through Pinto's body when he heard the sound of splitting timber and the squeaking sound of rusty hinges. Incantations at the grave side evoked the strangest uproar within the grave. An impatient guttural voice questioned the reason for such a rude awakening and threatened a costly reprisal.

Pinto's purpose of the invocation was to locate the whereabouts of Samoo so as to seek his revenge personally, and in that respect he was prepared to go to the ends of the earth. Indeed, Samoo's whereabouts was traced within the next few days as directed by the evil spirit of the notorious murderer. He was found dead in an obscure ditch covered with overgrown bamboo. The cause of his death remained a mystery and, like everything else, it was all forgotten in the course of time.

In the circumstances, Pinto was deprived of the opportunity for vengeance. Moreover, his terrifying experience at the graveyard had left him in a permanent state of shock. He was, all in all, mentally deranged.

This story was in fact told to me by a village elder who had witnessed in horror Samoo's and Pinto's last game of cards, had seen their last fight. Not long after that, both Samoo and Pinto were dead. It was believed that Samoo had carried out an invocation at the same grave prior to Pinto's visit.

24

Frolic at Rum Shop

In the same way as Washing Day at the Hot Springs provided an outlet for the women to air their views on day to day topics, the rum shop served a similar purpose for a great number of men in the village. They regularly gathered at the rum shop on Saturday afternoons. It was the only shop in the village at that time and therefore stocked general household goods as well; the men, however, confined themselves to the wine and spirits department. Highlights of the following incidents will suffice to illustrate the nature of events which generally occurred.

One by one the men strolled casually into the rum shop. Each received a hearty and boisterous welcome from the proprietor, Mr Gomez, gloating in anticipation of a good patronage. The men gathered early for whatever concession there might have been on that day for early customers. After initial inhibitions were washed down by preliminary toasts of good health, an assertive voice rang out.

'Come on Luther, drink up, drink up!'

Mr Bishop, a large forceful character, was in fact, expressing his disapproval of Luther's sluggish consumption of his beverage.

'Are you in a great hurry, Mr Bishop? . . . The day is still young as far as I can make out,' Luther uttered with unmistakable indifference and leisurely sipping his potent 'nectar'.

There was a death-like hush as the implications of Luther's response was being carefully appraised. But Luther's remark was full of innocence for he said what had come to him naturally, in order to slow down the pace of intoxication. During this uneasy pause however, Luther began to wonder what he had let himself into, for Mr Bishop was bad-tempered, with a great deal of influence. Moreover he was tall and muscular, Luther was short and slightly built.

'Come, come, come on Luther, drink up!' Mr Bishop commanded as he brought down his heavy fist upon the table and immediately emptied the contents of his glass with a quick backward jerk of the head for snappish accommodation.

Luther nearly jumped out of his pants. His beady eyes had taken the distended throbbing blood vessels on Mr Bishop's forehead that he was in a vexatious mood. Luther's predicament was heightened by the fact that he was short of cash and couldn't stand the next round of drinks. However, he struck upon a plan.

'Mr Bishop, I can't drink anymore on an empty stomach. If you care to come to my place we can have a good meal there with lots of drink as well,' he assured Mr Bishop.

Here again there was an uneasy silence, then Mr Bishop, smiling broadly, accepted the invitation. But immediately, a cheerful call rang out from Mr Gomez at the top of the stairs. He had seen from the window on the first floor the well-known figure of Danny on his way towards the shop. Being previously a regular customer, Mr Gomez was overflowing with joy.

'Hey! Hey everybody, come . . . see who's here . . . it's Danny at last. Let's give him a warm welcome. Come on now, drinks on the house,' he proclaimed.

167

Mr Gomez had overheard Luther's conversation with Mr Bishop on the matter of their imminent departure; hence his seemingly kind gesture was intended to prevent the 'big spender' in the personage of Mr Bishop from leaving the rum shop. The appearance of Danny on the scene at that time was merely a coincidence. Thus, at one fell swoop Mr Gomez had obtusely managed to boost his image and his sales by pernicious practices of seductive camaraderie.

It is a great pity that the old saying: 'When a man is down keep him down,' seemed to have attained universal acceptance. And what's more, it does not necessarily apply to the protagonists involved in a particular issue. Let's take Danny's case for example:

Danny was a kindly man of small stature in his early forties. Guilty and ashamed of his drinking habits, he struggled desperately to refrain from visiting the rum shop.

'I must avoid getting myself into a position where Mr Gomez and some of my so-called friends would make me a laughing-stock again,' Danny said to himself over and over following a very unsettling incident at the rum shop in the recent past. He was succeeding until at last, the slowly-built pressure at his home reached explosion point.

'Danny, I'm getting . . . in fact I'm fed up with you hanging around me in the kitchen noon and night,' remarked Gurty, his wife, in outrage.

'That's not true, Gurty and you know that . . . I've been trying to help you.'

'I don't need your help; I want some fresh air about the place.'

'Well, what you want me to do, Gurty?' asked Danny.

'You suit yourself, but don't hang around me; I can't breathe when you're around. Why don't you go fishing, hunting, crab catching or something. . . ?'

'You must be getting stupid, this is not crab season,' Danny emphasised, sniggering furtively. In her fury, with surprising agility, she spun round, clutched Danny's shirt – a fist full of it – at chest height and jerkily pushed him backwards against a partition in the kitchen. From a shelf above his head were utensils swinging like pendulums, they not only posed a threat to his safety but offered him means of retaliation should he succumb to the temptation.

As Danny reached up to clear a view from behind the curtain of frying-pans, his fleet-footed missis, in the twinkling of an eye, grabbed his upraised hand and hitched him up into a half-nelson. While subjecting him to constant abuse, his wife virtually frog-marched him to their front door where she gave him a final pasting with the said frying-pan on his backside before throwing him out. She then gently locked the door and retired for her afternoon sleep.

With his wife at twice his weight and much taller than he, she had overwhelming advantage. In addition, her agility of tongue and body outclassed Danny's by far. And so in his predicament – a catch twenty-two, or similarly, a choice between the devil and the deep blue sea; he chose what he thought to be the lesser of the two evils and wended his way back to the rum shop.

Also after that bewildering ovation given to him on his revisit to the rum shop, he felt totally rejuvenated and concluded that life was worth living after all. Everyone in the village knew of his domestic problems and hastened to succour him generously.

But, Danny had his pride, hence he felt obliged to stand at least one round of drinks. Delving into his pockets one by one, he realized that he hadn't sufficient cash to meet the requirement. As he lifted up his eye from his empty glass he caught sight of Mr Gomez looking in his direction and beckoned him over. 'There is only one thing to do,' he said to himself. . . . 'Ask Mr Gomez for credit,' he concluded.

Good-looking, tall, well-built and of Portuguese descendant, Mr Gomez glided across in business-like fashion towards Danny.

Resting his elbows on the counter in a customary manner, he said quietly to Danny, 'Now tell me what I can do for you, what is it you want?' he remarked in a loud voice, half-jokingly.

Surprised by the sudden change of attitude, somewhat subdued, Danny said, 'Can I speak to you for a moment, privately?'

Mr Gomez stood back and laughing aloud, said to the customers, 'Hey, hey, listen to this everybody! I am here on business and Danny here, wants me to speak with him privately?' What is this all about? We're here to enjoy ourselves together . . . no secrets, please. So come on, Danny speak up please, we're listening . . . all eyes on you,' Mr Gomez asserted as he looked around mockingly amidst great laughter.

Just then Molino, a notorious knife-fighter, attracted by the apparent hilarity, walked into the rum shop to find out what it was all about. The laughter ceased immediately upon his entry for he was well-known as the defender of the weak.

After a slight pause, Molino, glancing around said, 'I don't know whether this is a private party or not; I heard the laughter and I wondered what it was all about. Would someone care to tell me?' he asked.

Nobody replied.

Scanning the room, his eyes fell upon Danny who now seemed helpless.

Molino walked up to him and said, 'I remember you . . . you're not fit to be here, come on, I'll accompany you home.'

As they were leaving the rum shop Molino looked around and said, 'I'll soon be back.'

The uncharitable plight of the weak and helpless as exemplified in the foregoing Rum Shop episode is extensively illustrated the world over; and not only in the affair of human relationship but also in other living creatures. For example, in my experience during childhood, the stunted pig of an otherwise healthy litter was often left behind or pushed aside at feed time. Or in the case of a retarded bantam of an otherwise healthy brood, inflicted with pocks and yaws, it was invariably set upon by all and sundry including brothers and sisters.

Of course Charles Robert Darwin, the English naturalist – early nineteenth century – gave us much to think about on the subject of Natural Selection. But the practice of gross neglect in many instances, and even blatant ridicule at the plight of the unfortunate, augurs unfavourably for future generations. And, of course, the matter is compounded when there is not even a glimmer of compunction on the part of the perpetrators.

25

Carnival Dance – Coronation of King and Queen

As a musician, even though only as hobby, I was frequently caught up in the tide of events; sometimes against my instinctive inclinations. Here is a case in point.

I was twenty-one and had already attained the reputation of being one of the most promising jazz clarinettist in the south of the country. I did not relish the acclaim nor did I pay any heed to it whatsoever, since my main interest was directed to improving myself at work. Surprisingly, one Sunday morning a passenger in a hired car called from a nearby town, four miles away, at our house in desperation. It was at the height of carnival preparations and he called to ask my favour. I answered the door.

'Good morning, I'm looking for Jacob, the clarinettist, does he live here?'

'Yes I'm Jacob,' I replied.

'Oh, thank heavens, man, I've been looking for you all over the place.'

Patrice, the wide-eyed messenger, about twenty-six, brown complexioned, tall, lean and slightly hunched, told me of the calamity with which his band leader was faced. He was the deputy band leader and was charged with the responsibility of finding a suitable replacement for the band's ill-stricken clarinettist at all costs. They were scheduled to play at a very important celebration that very night. It turned out that the person I was expected to replace was known to be one of the island's finest performers on the clarinet.

In the circumstances, I was much more reluctant than I might have been otherwise, and Patrice spent over fifteen minutes trying to convince me that my handling of the instrument was not unlike that of Charlie Windsor for whom I was being asked to deputise.

Continuing the process he said, 'Look here, man, this is the most important night of the whole carnival. You could make a good name for yourself and good money besides.'

'Really, I'm not interested in either of those things,' I said.

'Then why hesitate? We'll arrange your transport back home, of course. What do you say?'

I thought to myself: A country lad . . . to be suddenly taken to a big town to take the place of a musician of Charlie Windsor's reputation was no easy task to contemplate. Moreover, The Windjammer, a celebrated dance hall, had a reputation of its own. I was indeed very reluctant to accept the invitation.

I suddenly reflected upon the fact that I was twenty-one, and felt that I should exert myself a little more, so after a brief consultation with a close elder relative in another room, I decided in favour of accepting the invitation.

Patrice was delighted and his eyes blinked over and over, clutching my arm in an awkward attempt to do a little dance in appreciation. He then suggested that we leave immediately for San Fernando, the second largest town in the country at that time.

In response to my enquiry as to why it was necessary to leave so promptly, he explained that it would give us time for some rehearsals on the spot, and moreover, to meet Bill Morando, the band leader and other members of the team.

173

Patrice then shuffled into his pockets and took out a wad of dollar notes. He offered to pay me for my services in advance, but I refused to accept and made it clear that I played the clarinet as a hobby, and was not prepared to be held under contract. After some deliberation, we set off for San Fernando in a pre-carnival atmosphere, in the motor car which he had retained for the purpose.

I asked Patrice for a list of the pieces of music which they intended to play that evening, and I looked through it in some detail on our way to the town. I was acquainted with most pieces, and the key in which they were written. I felt, therefore, quite at ease.

We had covered the four miles to San Fernando in a shorter space of time than I had anticipated, and were taken to Patrice's home where three other musicians were waiting. Among them was Pascaro, a talented musician of great versatility. He was very affable and of refined demeanour. We immediately struck up a good relationship, and realizing that I was an absolute greenhorn so far as town and city atmosphere was concerned, he instinctively undertook to shepherd me along.

Pascaro almost twice my age had played every stringed instrument I knew of, including the harp. He had lived in the capital city in the north for several years and had played in several of the city's most prestigious jazz bands. He played the tenor banjo, with one of the best bands in the south at the time.

He was a man of average height with a pleasing countenance that charged the atmosphere around him with animation. His general expression reflected an enduring contentment derived from the pleasure he enjoyed by adapting to the necessities of everyday life. His light-brown complexion, golden, curly hair and flashing bluish-grey eyes made him very outstanding. His deportment and manner of speech reflected a degree of refine-

174

ment and education which I believed were unusual for someone in such environment. Maybe he had a similar impression of me.

We arrived at the dance hall on the Sunday evening, well ahead of time and Patrice leisurely completed the stage arrangements, with music stands in the appropriate places. Immediately afterwards, the band leader arrived, and after a formal introduction, we seated ourselves in our respective places on the stage.

Within a few moments, the band struck up with one of the most popular tunes of the session. Appropriately, it was a calypso, for the following two days, Monday and Tuesday, had been declared public carnival holidays. At 6 p.m. the grand carnival dance and celebrations will have begun. It was for this prestigious occasion that I was chosen to join the famous band of musicians, for an all-night session: 6 p.m.-6 a.m.

Within a short while, large crowds began to swarm into the room, and the appreciation of the music was openly expressed by their enthusiastic applause. There were many among them who thought that Charles Windsor had recovered from his illness. I had not realized that the master clarinettist had been unwell for some weeks. I was praised by the band leader and his deputy, but above all, by Pascaro whose musicianship ranked highest of all in my estimation.

The carnival atmosphere had been steadily gathering momentum and as the evening progressed, more and more people appeared in fancy dresses, signifying that a general build-up was in progress. Somewhat puzzled, I asked Pascaro what it was all about. He informed me that the elected King and Queen of Carnival would be crowned in the hall at midnight; hence the whole celebration was being built up to that highlight.

It was now approaching 11.45 p.m. and several onlookers had begun to gather around the musicians' stage, seemingly to ensure the maintenance of a rousing tempo. Pascaro had moved closer to me and warned me not to let up, especially at the crucial moment.

As the crowd continued to swell the room, I realized that the crucial moment was near at hand. It had now turned 11.50 p.m. and a flood of scantily-dressed women and oddly-dressed men, all in bright colourful garments, surged into the hall.

The band leader suddenly switched to a more erotic piece of much quicker tempo. The whole band followed without a hitch, and the crowd roared with excitement. I was at the height of my greatest versatility with the clarinet, and rather enjoyed the challenge.

Suddenly, about a dozen able-bodied men in uniform entered the fully opened doorway and cleared the crowd away from the centre of the hall. A signal was flashed from the entrance, a change of music greeted the dancing lady. She danced her way through the human corridor at the entrance into the hall, and fanned out in free-style in the centre, and up to the dance band amidst rousing applause. At the flash of another signal, a heightened round of applause emerged, and a male dancing figure made his spectacular entry.

And now, with non-stop music and a clear space in the centre of the hall, the elected King at one end, and the Queen at the other began dancing towards each other, directly and indirectly, to the most evocative piece of music I had ever heard. And it was to this special music, with its broken and off-beat rhythm, that the freelance couple danced towards each other, showing off, pretending to be shy and innocent strangers.

Fernando, twenty-eight, black, sturdy with rippling muscles, tall, unsmiling with gleaming eyes set on the Queen, seemed menacingly purposeful.

On the other hand, the heroine of about twenty-six, and slighter, shorter than the King and outstandingly shapely, nimbly angled her way around him with the most provocative of whimsical dances and glances.

In her exquisitely tempting manner, Queen Nicola captured the hearts of the crowd. Her glistening black skin oozing with perspiration, seemed to add lustre to her vibrant performance, and accentuated the highlights of her female form. And King Fernando, in a similar way, made his own indelible impressions.

These marvellous dancers were now about ten feet apart, made their approach towards each other, with impulsive expressions of fantasy.

The sweltering crowd roared and shouts of 'Music! Music! Music!' echoed around the room. I realized that my attention had been distracted, and I dare say, other members of the band were struck likewise. But were less affected. They were seasoned players in such atmosphere.

But now, with renewed impetus, the heavy beat of the drums and double-bass enlivened the whole proceedings to a height which I had never before experienced.

The dancers, now about six feet apart, moving gradually closer and closer towards each other, in a frenzied dance of sexual posturings, the like of which I had never imagined the human being to have been capable. The more pendulous aspects of their bodies sprang into an exceptional pulsating vivacity as the syncopated music reverberated around the hall.

A tumultuous applause greeted their eventual embrace, and their graceful expression of gratitude and delight had silenced the audience for a fleeting moment . . . and another rousing burst of applause ensued.

Their glittering crowns, trimmed red and gold with dangling multicoloured ribbons added to their enchantment. A brief proclamation in their honour by an official had brought the particular ceremony to a close, and the crowd joined into a unified band of merry-makers.

On several occasions, I was dazed with disbelief. My eyes were opened. In that comparatively brief period of revelry, I had seen much and heard a lot . . . that famous dance hall – The Windjammer – was positively jammed tight that night.

26

City Carnival

The most spectacular events of the carnival festivities were
staged on the Tuesday, the second (last) day of the festival;
and it was well-known that Port-of-Spain, the capital city,
held the greatest attraction. In the wake of my staggering
adventure, I became more curious about celebrations in the
city, and wanted to know too how my playing of the clarinet
compared with the top clarinettists in the north.

Rosina, a very beautiful and sprightly city girl of
twenty-three, was born in Central America. She was
working on a field study for her post-graduate work, and
coverage of Carnival in Trinidad was one of her subjects.
Ten days after her arrival she journeyed down from the
city on a special invitation to witness the well-publicised
Coronation Dance in the south of the country.

The manner in which she frequently glanced at the
band, I suspected she was musical, and this proved to be
correct at the end of the function.

'Excuse me, Senor, . . . Mister,' she said gliding her
way, smiling gaily in her approach towards me. I listened
attentively. 'I say something . . . you don't mind, no?'

'Oh, not at all, what is it?' I asked, in a bold manner
being conscious of the fact that I was now a grown-up. I
was of course mannerly in my reply.

'I only want to say . . . the orchestra . . . the music is all
good, and you play the clarinet very well.'

179

'Thank you, thank you for all of us,' I added, glancing round to the other members of the band. 'Tell me, I suppose you play a musical instrument yourself, what is it you play?'

'I play the piano these days, but I used to play the clarinet . . . too hard for me,' she remarked with bright searching eyes and a charming smile.

On further acquaintance, she explained that she would be returning to the city that very Monday night in order to ensure that she misses nothing of the following day – the best of the carnival.

'But you coming to the city too, yes? At moment, my friend, working together, couldn't come to this country with me, so. . . ,' Rosina remarked as she shrugged her shoulders.

'We could meet somewhere in the city if you like that, yes?'

I hesitated.

'Well, the idea sounds good, but I've never been to the city during the carnival celebrations. Moreover, I don't know the city well,' I asserted.

'Ah, that's a good reason to it . . . we not children now. We'll find out,' she asserted.

During that brief encounter, I succumbed to Rosina's irresistible charm and persuasion and accepted her invitation. We arranged a rendezvous in the city for 11 a.m. on the Tuesday.

Rosina was of Spanish descent. She was looking the other way as I approached our rendezvous and I doubted that she could have looked as radiant as she did. As she turned sideways, her profile revealed such statistics as may have courted the envy of the top model of the day. Fair and slightly taller than average, her wide-brimmed white hat with a red band matched her red and white polka-dot skirt, twirling innocently by a cool breeze. I paused without realizing it, wondering whether she was the same girl with whom I'd spoken the previous day.

At that moment she seemed so close and yet so far away, for there were bands on parade and she took no notice, appearing to look to a distant horizon. I continued walking towards her and as she turned in my direction it was as though a chord in a mighty symphony had been struck with such eloquence that took me beyond the boundaries of her gaze. I momentarily experienced a strange feeling of complete absence.

She gasped in surprise and her sparkling eyes gleamed with welcome.

'Hello! You caught the early train after all. I'm so glad,' Rosina remarked with great excitement.

Then her pouted rose-coloured lips relaxed into a most affectionate smile. I was all but frozen.

Her red hooped earrings dangled attractively as we walked leisurely, hand in hand, to a nearby restaurant where we refreshed ourselves and planned the course of the day. As she ran her fingers across her necklace, I couldn't help admiring the pendant, contrasting beautifully with her fair complexion. I had time to observe too, her fingernails, necklace, earrings and hatband were quite similar in colour, exquisitely harmonious.

I was shown the house in which she was staying temporarily, then we visited some of the high spots before moving on to the focus of attention where the various bands gathered to contest the prizes. I had never imagined the extent of preparations that were involved in the promotion of the various bands. I realized only then that many of the bands were truly representative of major historical events which occurred in various parts of the world centuries ago and, of course, in more recent times.

Current events, too, were fully represented. It was only then, also, that I became aware of the amount of research that was necessary to produce such realistic displays as I had seen. The costumes I saw at first-hand demanded great skill, patience and ingenuity on the part of the designer, craftsman and craftswoman.

The calypso music which accompanied the bands were of the latest composition. The lyrics displayed diverse poetic talent, frequently unrecognised or unappreciated by the vast majority of members of the public. The combined effect of music, singing and dancing charged the atmosphere with tremendous excitement as the various bands slowly made their way to the prize-giving centres.

At brief interludes, Rosina and I joined the hustle and bustle, in the thick of it all. As the afternoon began to slip away, the serious thought of work the following day entered my mind.

Departure arrangements – times and the particular railway station – had been left to Rosina. It was agreed then that I should catch the last train from the city, scheduled to leave at 10.30 p.m. After tea in a restaurant near Marine Square, as it was known, Rosina went back to her relations allegedly to discuss an urgent matter she'd overlooked. We'd planned to meet at the appropriate platform at 10.15.

I arrived well on time but the last train departed at 10. Moments later Rosina arrived, seemingly in a flurry but not particularly concerned that we had missed the last train. My dismay and disappointment were sharply registered. I'd never slept away from home before, and I was certain that I did not have enough money to pay for any form of lodgings in the city.

'Don't be mad with me, and don't look so worried either,' Rosina remarked. 'You can't always rely on the times of the train so I made arrangements just in case . . . come with me,' she added in a docile tone of appeasement,

182

as she glanced at me for a sympathetic response.

But I was glassy-eyed and accompanied her like a lamb, back into the centre of town and into an alleyway. There she knocked on a strange door which creaked mournfully on opening as a shady frail figure furtively beckoned us in, and led us to a small single bedroom on the first floor. It seemed very obvious that we had been expected. The whole atmosphere was totally foreign to me, and I was very much ill at ease.

Rosina hastened the sleeping arrangements while I stood still pretending to look at a picture on the wall, thinking: Here I am with hardly any choice . . . my first night away from home, locked in a room with a girl completely undressed and already in bed, urging me to get in with her.

'Why don't you come in? We don't want to miss the first train in the morning as well! You'll be well in time for work . . . come on,' she urged coaxingly with an arm outstretched from beneath a transparent netting bed-cover. She was completely naked indeed. I was completely overwhelmed by her beauty and boldness. I was utterly speechless.

'You know, I think you're unfair; why are you so miserable . . . and mad with me for missing your train?' she remarked after a period of silence. 'You know it wasn't my fault that you missed your train, and even so, I told you that I was sorry more than a thousand times already. So what you want me to do now?' she asked in frustration.

'Nothing, just leave me alone!' I replied appealingly.

After a short pause she muttered, 'And I arranged for us to have such a nice time here together . . . alone with each other. And you can catch the early train back home in time for work in the morning.'

Her voice, strong at first, sank to a mere whisper as she gently removed the netting cover and sat up at the front edge of the bed, still unclothed, with her head supported by cupped hands and elbows resting on her thighs. She seemed truly repentant. Standing fully dressed, a few yards away, still pondering over my predicament, I heard a stir and I turned towards her.

She was now standing upright with arms hanging limply at her side. Slowly and steadfastly, she advanced towards me. I had never been confronted with such a situation, and indeed had not seen the unclothed body of an adult female before, let alone in motion. I was too stunned to move. As she continued her slow advance, my eyes instinctively flickered, darting from one to another, and another, and another . . . of the highlights of her femininity. My annoyance and disappointments at having missed the last train home that night had gradually dissipated.

Rosina, with her sensuous lips deliberately pouting, continued her approach towards me very slowly now, and placing her arms on my shoulders, one on each side, interlocked her fingers behind my neck, and began swaying gently to the evocative beat of the most popular calypso music of the day.

'Come to bed,' she urged, 'Come on, come on . . . let us. . . ,' she prompted urgently but coaxingly.

As she let go of my neck and inched her way back towards the bed, wobbling gracefully before me, she revealed yet new and staggering dimensions of the female form.

As we neared the bed, suddenly, as though by agreement, all the lights in the building went out, leaving only a faint glimmer in the corner of the room. The numerous chatterings came almost to an abrupt end, and unfamiliar bed-noises gradually began to erupt all around – from the floor above and adjacent rooms.

The carnival celebrations officially came to an end at

midnight on the Tuesday, and although the lights were put out to mark the end, a new energetic form of activity had only just begun with rapturous rumblings everywhere.

Stimulated by the obvious state of excitement, Rosina tossed aside her net covering, sprang out of bed and rushed to me as I stood looking at a book on the table. I turned quickly towards her, and caught a fleeting glimpse of her natural form once more.

I was delightfully astonished and before I had time to think, she threw both arms around my neck and pulled me close, very close to her. The suddenness of the engagement had caught me off balance, and my arms inadvertently folded around her, just above the small of her back.

We both appeared to be a little surprised at this rapid development, but Rosina did not relax her embrace around my shoulders. She began to breathe as though short of breath. I relaxed my hold of her and my hands slipped down, beyond the small of her back to a natural resting place where, instinctively, they loitered motionless.

Rosina seemed restless and made several utterances of endearment, 'Come, let's go to bed now so you can catch the first train to San Fernando early in the morning.'

She kept moving, wriggling and moving about all the time, as she continued to make inaudible remarks in my ears as though in secret. I was being overwhelmed, and my mind suddenly flashed back to some of the things I had heard, while remaining helplessly frozen in my predicament.

I had heard men, experienced men, speak about some of the goings-on in many hotels they had visited, and heard of the manner of certain girls that sickened them. Having been caught up in a situation that so much

185

resembled their description, I shuddered at the thought of being a likely victim. Thus I found it impracticable to bolt out from mind the possibility of such occurrences, to my detriment. In addition, I had heard of the presence of gambling dens in such buildings, and of police raids.

Should there be such a raid, I feared that it would result in a mass arrest, and I would be implicated with gamblers and prostitutes. I dreaded and despised every aspect of the whole situation and yet I felt utterly incapable of dealing with the matter in a creditable fashion.

Later that night, when the raucous din in the streets had subsided, one had to contend with, what were to me then, weird and unfamiliar sounds within the building itself, seemingly from rooms all around and again from above. Alarming sounds odd beds and floorboards in motion, and moans and groans persisted as undertones in concert with the continuous strains of music, song and wild laughter. And there was dancing too.

This form of so-called revelry had set me deeper in thought, and I recalled many other things I had heard about sleeping out in such places.

Mattresses laden with bed bugs and lice, and worst of all, the possibility of contracting all sorts of diseases by close association with the opposite sex. How close an association, and what manner of association, I did not know at the time, but I considered it safer to keep my distance.

With so many gruesome thoughts chasing one another around my head, it was imperative that I suppressed the impulses that were being generated within me by the exhilarating cosiness in which I was closeted. My emotional conflict was becoming unbearable, and I fervently prayed for some form of escape.

Immediately, I sensed the onset of a transformation and a gradual disengagement of my close contact with

Rosina. I do not recall any conversation there may have been, and I have no recollection of how I came to be lying on the floor, fully clothed beside the bed, although I'd given the idea some consideration beforehand.

Rosina was sound asleep, and I realized the opportunity of being able to make a dash for it in case of any emergency. Moreover, being in that state of readiness, I had minimised the menace of lice and bed bugs. Mice, however, were undeterred by my intrusion. The entire floor was their playground, I was certain. All in all, I rested quite well and looked forward to the train journey home and my day's work ahead.

I had just awakened from a light sleep when the clock in the church tower nearby struck four. It was about that time in the morning that I intended to leave for the railway station, in order to avoid the heavy traffic during rush hour. After collecting my senses for a few moments, I slowly rose to my feet and found myself glancing down at Rosina, fast asleep on the bed, as she was one hour ago when I last glanced at her.

As much as I wanted to make a quick departure lest I awakened her, I was compelled to wait yet awhile. In the warmth of the night, she had cast aside her netting cover instinctively; and in her nudity was charm and magnanimity. She was breathing heavily and I could not help noticing the slow rise and fall of her bosom. I reflected on the 'breath of life', with many of its complexities.

I saw Rosina as a magnificent example of womanhood. There was a hallowing gentleness about her and I prayed that no harm would ever attend her. Just then, an alarming sound erupted some distance away and seemed to be advancing rapidly. It sounded very much like the siren of a police car and I was not prepared to find out. Thus, with fleet of foot and sleight of hand, I quickly unlocked the door and dashed out into the corridor. I had written a note earlier thanking Rosina for her delightful companionship.

Pausing for a few moments to locate the sound of the siren, I was greatly relieved to realize that it was receding and not heading my way after all, but I could not re-enter the room I'd occupied. I was automatically locked out.

The habit of getting up early had served me in good stead. Thus, I was able to make an early departure ensuring that Rosina was undisturbed. On my way to the railway station, I walked along the seafront and reflected upon the various aspects of my adventure, and the familiar cries of seagulls in the cool breeze of dawn reminded me of those at Campeche Bay, with the realisation that seagulls are the same everywhere.

I arrived at the station with several minutes to spare, and deliberately chose a seat so as to face the direction of the hotel in which I spent the night. I hoped, somehow, that in so doing, I would recapture at least, the highlights of the fleeting raptures I had experienced during my stay in the evocative atmosphere of the bedroom on the first floor.

In many ways, it had been a bewildering fascination far beyond my comprehension. All my encounters with Rosina that carnival night at an hotel in the city were both acutely painful and acutely pleasurable – extensively evocative exceeding by far all conceivable motions I may have had such a venture. A state of suspended animation had obstinately asserted itself with teasing and tormenting in a case of what was 'to be or not to be'. The latter was of the spirit and so Rosina was left sound asleep.

All those things I experienced afresh between spells of sleep and daydream in those early hours of the morning on the express train back to my village home. I knew that Matosh, one of my cousins, two years my senior, would say to me, 'Ah, there you are! Went to the big city for

Carnival, eh? . . . stayed the night as well, I understand. All right! All right, city guy!'

'That's right,' I would reply curtly, knowing him to be of the jealous nature.

Indeed I met Matosh on the cricket field on the Wednesday evening, the same day of my return from the city; we were left behind gathering up the implements.

'How did you get on then?' Matosh asked. 'After your big night out?' he added.

'How . . . what do you mean?'

'Well, you stayed the night, didn't you? Didn't you?' he repeatedly asserted, pushing me back sharply with his half-clenched fist against my chest, insisting on a reply, half-smiling.

Matosh was about my build, but he was a little more robust. Not having been in close contact during that period, our views were somewhat dissimilar. In those days elder relatives, even by two years, asserted their authority upon their juniors, sometimes sneakily, especially if there were underlying elements of jealousy. And Matosh may well have had cause for that, I gathered from his various remarks.

'You're lucky, aren't you!' he remarked several times.

'What makes you think so?' I replied.

'I can see, I know about girls, you know. Besides, I heard fellows say that girls like you.'

'Well, I can tell you that I've had nothing to do with. . . .'

'Oh yes, you have,' asserted Matosh, sharply interrupting the conversation. 'Girls flock round you because you play the clarinet and run the village band. You know that, don't you? . . . Don't you?' he insisted, as he advanced towards me, pushing with half-clenched fist against my chest, as he had done before.

I continued to back away, but he followed up with sharp thrusts against my stomach.

189

I protested angrily. 'Stop your nonsense, Matosh!' I exclaimed as I parried his attempt.

That rather infuriated him, and discarding the cricket implements we had begun collecting, he stood back and said, 'Well, then, let's have it out fair and square.'

I always did all I could to avoid squabbles, and fights in particular, but in an aggressive boxing stance, he rushed towards me and reached out for my face with his left hand. He had charged with a long sweep of the arm, thus I saw it coming a long way off and parried successfully, as I continued to back away. And now before I could blink my eyes, he landed a stinging blow with his left hand on my right cheek. I was astounded but it alerted me in knowing what to expect. Yet, there was another quick delivery, and yet another, and also another, also in like manner.

It was obvious that I had no defence for the onslaught and so I decided to attack in the manner I felt suitable of protecting myself. He had sensed my determination and had begun to throw both hands at me. With a mad rush, I tore through his defence and at a very close range, delivered two lightning butts on the nose. Maddened by the droplets of blood, he fought desperately to ward me off, but I'd tied him up in a clench at which, fortunately, I was pretty good.

Scowling and grunting in the grapple, we sought for advantage, circling one way and then the other. As soon as he appeared to be gaining the upper hand, I broke off suddenly. At that momentary disruption of his concentration, I threw him heavily to the ground and swiftly pinned him there, in a notorious clench.

All I was concerned about at that moment was preventing him from hitting me such stinging blows, and that I'd found a way of stopping him. He must have been in agony for I was nearly deafened by his yells and groans. He had weakened considerably and the deep sound of a growling dog rapidly came to the scene of our contest and suddenly ended the affray.

The owner of the dog soon appeared. Matosh and I received a severe warning but were spared the dreaded consequences of revealing the matter to our relatives and friends.

It was all the result of a reaction from which jealousy had gradually built up over the years, and the occasion of a country boy attending Carnival festivities in the city in those days was too much for Matosh to endure in any other way.

Judging from the result of the encounter, I felt certain that Matosh would have a greater regard for me in the future. I was correct in my assessment.

27

Odd Encounter

Several months after that incident, Matosh showed a great appreciation of my company, and befriended me with a form of humility and respect which was quite embarrassing at times. Even in those youthful days it occurred to me that my father had made the most of the educational facilities available on the family's behalf. I had no extra tuition, but was never kept away from school. My occupation as a draughtsman with field surveying experience placed me above average in the eyes of the community, apart from my eldest and youngest brothers who were established members of the teaching profession.

Matters of elegance, beauty and refinement – everything uplifting – had always appealed to me, and no doubt my contact with the more refined elements in the drawing office had enhanced that inclination. I was aware of an improvement in my deportment, too, and I took great pains to subdue it along with some other refinement lest it be said that I was 'playing Englishman', because the Chief Draughtsman was an Englishman.

In fact, it was my fear of such a rumour that decided me not to distance myself too much from the ordinary run of the mill. I was satisfied with my judgement as to where the line should be drawn. Thus, when Matosh sought my assistance in great confidence some weeks after our physical encounter on the cricket field, I agreed to rally to his aid.

Matosh's sister had taken ill and after a fortnight appeared to be dying. Believing it was unnatural, he decided to seek the intervention of a so-called bushman. This was a matter strictly against the law and, as usual, I was in disagreement with the course of action. He pleaded with me to accompany him deep into the bush where he had located the recluse in advance.

'I'm not used to this sort of thing you know,' I said.

'Jacob, look here, man; look here! It's a matter of life or death. I understand your position but I can't get anyone to come with me, that's why I'm pleading with you,' he exclaimed.

'What exactly do you want me to do?'

'Nothing!' he said.

'You mean there's nothing to do, yet you need my help.'

'Oh it's only for the company. I'll do the talking.'

Fearing that I would be held responsible should his sister die, I undertook the trek with him.

Despite my decision to accompany him on his mission, two factors worried me greatly: my fear of the police, and the nagging thought that Matosh was inclined to dabble in witchcraft. But I was determined to do all I could to help his dying sister.

Thus, before dawn on the morning in question, we set off on our bicycles for a distance of about three miles on nicely surfaced road, followed by two miles on a rough dirt surface which led off to a narrow grassy track. Matosh led the way furtively, along the track with thick grass and shrubbery, angling and weaving precariously to evade the obstacles imposed by overhanging branches heavily dew-laden. There was, however, no escape from the wet grass and bushes which we knew, of course, would dry out from our clothes within moments in the sunlight. After a distance of about 500 yards we abandoned our cycles, hid them carefully in the bushes and continued the remaining mile with minimum obstruction.

However, there was an alarming incident as we approached our destination. I was never at ease for one moment during this venture, and I began to think of means of making my escape should the police be hiding somewhere in wait. No sooner than these thoughts had run through my mind than a sudden rustling of leaves erupted about two yards or so ahead of us. We stopped abruptly and, without saying a word, Matosh slowly turned round and looked at me. I was very close behind him.

The branches of a blacksage tree slowly parted, and we saw a red-eyed man in black, standing still; but his eyes rolled to and fro, covering us both in his gaze. Now there were three of us standing motionless. He was in plain clothes. After a few agonising moments, he nimbly stepped out before us and a smile on the face of this quiet man immediately dispelled our anxiety. It was only then that we began to appreciate the beautiful song of the birds and the lovely scent of flowers in the morning air.

'Where are you going?' he asked as he stood in our path, more serious and red-eyed than a moment ago.

'Oh, I've come to see the Guru on behalf of my sister,' replied Matosh.

'Why didn't she come with you?' he asked, still looking our way as he furtively looked around. It was only when Matosh explained the situation that we were allowed to advance, and had to follow him for almost 100 yards.

The quiet man was a lookout for the Guru Matosh wanted to see and, having explained the purpose of the visit, the quiet man checked that we were not being followed, then conducted us to the Guru's hut nearby. After being introduced to an interpreter, we were requested to sit on the floor with our legs crossed, facing the Guru who himself sat in a similar manner. Matosh and I had to leave our shoes outside the hut before explaining the purpose of the visit in detail to the interpreter who, in turn, at the appropriate moment, communicated the request to the Guru, like the quiet man he was of a dark complexion, average height, slight build and of Indian descent.

Following upon this, an intense silence ensued. After a few moments the Guru began muttering incoherently. His body and limbs began to quiver with an alarming intensity. His eyes were bloodshot like those of the quiet man. As the mumbling and the trembling grew more intense, his eyes seemed as though they were beginning to turn inside out. Suddenly an object held in his left hand was flicked upward. It struck the galvanised iron roof in the manner of a hard object. I did not hear it fall. Simultaneously, there was a deep dull thud close to our feet. The Guru, seemingly in a state of spasm, had jerkily bent over forward crashing his forehead like a thunderbolt upon the earthen floor. With arms stretched out, one at each side with palms barely touching the floor. He developed a rigorous twitching, switching from mumbling to a form of gibberish incantation.

After a few moments of that ritual, a brief period of calm ensued during which the Guru resumed his original posture, sitting upright before us on the floor. I did all I could to retain my composure. I was near the point of panic when I saw the terrifying transformation that had taken place. Now, Matosh and I had before us a completely strange, grotesque figure uncomfortably close, and speaking aloud in yet another tongue.

The interpreter was alert and intense and must have noted every word on paper. With this sequence over and done with, the Guru lurched forward once again and assumed the former position, but the thud of forehead upon the floor was less intense. As his face moved through an arc towards the floor, I sensed the full impact of the monstrosity. There was something alien about it all. I disliked the whole situation intensely. However, within a few moments an exhausted figure slowly sat up in the person of the Guru we saw in the first place. Tired and sweating profusely, he asked the interpreter to read out aloud the findings. The description of Matosh's sister, the position of the bed and the arrangement of other pieces of furniture in the house more than four miles away, were absolutely accurate.

Finally, the nature of the illness was disclosed. It was due to natural causes, and she would die within a week. Matosh was spellbound and so was I, but for reasons presumably quite different from those of Matosh. I did all I could to hasten the procedure and to be away from what I considered to be a dangerous episode zone, prone to police intervention. Four days later Matosh's sister was dead.

28

Village Sports

Immediately following my mother's death, evening life at home, particularly on Sundays, seemed lifeless and occasionally sad. My father often sat quietly on the rocking-chair that was once my mother's, sang sentimental songs and saddened himself to tears. They were songs they both knew and sang together several times over, and now he was singing them alone. And to make matters worse, he would end up singing their favourite hymns. On such occasions I was deeply saddened also. But his general outlook had always been bright and cheerful. So fortunately, the sad moments were only occasional, and grew more infrequent with the passage of time.

Of the five children in the family, a younger brother and I were the only two who lived at home with my father most of that period. It was not until two years or more before my father had fully recovered to his real self, so to speak. He was a quiet man of average height, sturdy, non-interfering and, in fact, a firm believer in minding his own business. That, of all things, was an advice he frequently repeated to our household: 'Mind your own business.'

During his brightest moments at home, after a function at which some alcoholic beverage was consumed, he often had our attention by singing to us and dancing to demonstrate what some of the old-time dances were like.

197

Even when we were in our teens, his habit of relating aspects of his past activities had continued. He had never been very overt, and so, every now and then, there would be something new and revealing, sometimes quite surprising – always interesting.

Somehow, I was of the impression that my father rather admired the donkey in an odd sort of way: 'Tricky and stubborn at times, but very reliable too . . . at times,' he would say, and then relate an incident in support of his remark.

For example, he related an incident in which one of his acquaintances was involved with his own donkey, named Trixo. In this case, I was given to understand, both donkey and owner were 'tricky'. It was on the occasion of the annual Village Fete, on the open playground. Nearly everyone in the village attended the Fete. My father and his friends were present in great numbers. They were in their mid-twenties at the time. Many visitors from neighbouring villages were present, as customary, and took part in the various fun and games.

On this particular occasion, a 'show off' from one of the neighbouring villages attended the Village Fete for the first time, and proclaimed himself a master donkey jockey. Crocker was the owner of Trixo, the tricky donkey in the village. He immediately challenged the stranger.

'Glad to have a sportsman of your stamp at our Village Fete, stranger. Let me introduce myself. My name is Crocker. What's yours?'

'Oh, everybody calls me Jaco -JACO-.' He spelt it out to Crocker.

'I heard you proclaim to be a Master Donkey rider.'

'No, sir. I *am* a Master Donkey Rider. There is no "proclaim" about that,' Jaco asserted.

'Well, I dare say, we'll soon find out how good you really are! That's providing you're man enough to accept a challenge.'

'Ah, but what is the challenge, Crocker . . . did you say your name is Crocker?'

'You sure right, man, everybody knows Crocker.'

'Well, what's the challenge? Oh, let me say this now – nothing doing without a wager,' said Jaco with a pompous smirk.

'Oh, don't worry; things are done proper here. Bagwandin here is the money man. He holds the wager and is the referee to boot,' said Crocker.

'Wait, hold on a minute; you haven't said what the wager is about and how much it is.'

'Ah, now you come to the point,' replied Crocker. 'Everyone here in the presence of the referee will bear witness. I, Crocker, bet you, Jaco, the sum of ten dollars that you cannot ride my donkey for longer than three minutes – that's to say you cannot stay on his back for longer than three minutes,' insisted Crocker.

Jaco burst out in laughter and ridicule: 'Man, you not serious! Come come; you joking . . . Where is the donkey. Bring it here, let me lay eyes on it!' Jaco demanded.

In an instant the donkey was brought on the scene, Jaco walked around with the keenest of eyes. He looks all right – slap the wager down. The challenge was accepted. A huge crowd gathered around and numerous side bets openly flourished. The starter was fired, voices raised, fluctuating in intensity with the skill and showmanship of the donkey rider.

The stranger nimbly sprung to his perch upon the donkey's back to the sound of tumultuous applause. He successfully dodged the animal's vicious biting attacks, to the cheers of his supporters, and now both rider and donkey paused, remaining still, each working out his next move. The crowd, too, remained still and quiet, very tense.

Then all of a sudden Trixo let fly with a series of high

kicks, taking the rider by surprise. But Jaco was a champion jockey, indeed, and survived it all. The crowd roared and began to cheer the stranger even more for his skill and first-class showmanship. Meanwhile Crocker, the owner of the donkey, fearing that his time was running out, disappeared, and was nowhere to be found.

Within about fifty seconds, the donkey remained still once more, then tried to sit down, or attempted to lie down, some believed. The crowd gasped, then immediately cheered as the rider averted the issue. Without pausing, Trixo began frisking about in a tight circle, and stopping suddenly. He tried to kneel down, but yet again the champion rider managed to hang on and pulled the animal back to order.

Huge crowds gathered from all over the playground, yelling and shouting with excitement. Time now seemed to be at an end, and all eyes began to cast glances at their watches. The donkey now took to prancing in his wildest mood, jerking the rider off balance. With a change to rough tactics, the rider tried to keep Trixo on a very tight rein.

The donkey tried once more to bite him again and again. Then out of the blue, at the height of enthusiasm, the donkey bolted out of the playground at a maddening pace. The crowd darted for safety.

No shouting, no pulling at the reins, in fact nothing that the stranger did had any effect of deterring the animal from retreating to his stable at speed, beneath a house built on stilts just high enough to accommodate the donkey – without a rider. It was Trixo's stable. The donkey had responded to his master's high-pitched whistle and returned home in absolute obedience. As for the stranger, a backward somersault in the nick of time had saved him from catastrophe, but with five seconds left to go he had lost the wager, and he dared not raise a hand in a strange village.

While on the subject of donkeys, it may be appropriate to relate yet another incident involving this animal. I was about ten years old. It was a very stormy evening and all the members of our family were already indoors.

It must have been about 7 o'clock in the evening. Streaks of lightning flashed through the flaws in the old wooden exterior wall of our house. The explosive sound of thunder that followed, rattled the galvanised iron roofing. Sustained heavy drumming of large raindrops, bursting on impact, seemingly tried to get at all who were dry and cosy in our house. It was at that moment, on reflecting upon one of his experiences at sea, that my father described the incident.

When he was a young man of about nineteen, he was a passenger on a schooner travelling from Port-of-Spain, the capital, to San Fernando, the largest town in the south of the island, some forty miles away. At about half-way along the journey a storm suddenly blew up and rose to such an intensity as alarmed the most seasoned seaman on board.

It was a two-masted schooner, regarded as a heavy-weight by islanders in those days, and yet it rolled and tossed and pitched, according to those who were familiar, or pretended to be familiar with the language of the sailing vessel. With no sign of improvement in the weather, and no possibility of sheltering at a nearby port, there was no option but to ride the storm.

He explained that some of the cargo – merchandise – had to be dumped overboard in great haste and orders to go below and batten down the hatches rang out repeatedly. Despite the repeated orders, my father explained that he could not bring himself to be shut in when he felt that he stood a better chance on deck. Thus, he furtively concealed himself on the deck and was subjected to considerable buffeting and other gross discomforts, but he stuck it out until the ship entered calmer waters, close to its destination. The storm by then had died down almost completely, he explained.

'But, Pa, those things they dumped overboard, could they have found them and picked them up after the storm?' I inquired.

'No, not really.'

'Why not, Pa?'

'Well, for one thing, there was no landmarks; we couldn't see anything, except some odd lights. And another thing, in rough waters like that all the cases and things would have drifted away by strong currents on the seabed.'

I observed my father smiling absentmindedly, as though reflecting upon the incident. I knew my father was a good swimmer, and wondered if he intended to swim ashore if the ship went down.

I asked him how would he have known where the land was in the dark.

'Pa, I know you are a good swimmer but do you think you would have been able to swim so far in the rough cold water? Apart from that, how would you have known where the land was in the dark, Pa?'

He then explained.

'Well, lad, I thought of all those things, I had my jack-knife with me and I kept my eye on a donkey in the far corner on the deck.'

'But what would you have done with the jack-knife, Pa?'

'Oh, cut the donkey free. It would have set off for the nearest land and I would have hung on to it somehow. In cases like that one can always trust a donkey', concluded my father, smiling confident that his faith in the trusted animal would have seen him through to safety.

When I was about twenty, in our village of Pointe-à-

Pierre, I was regarded as one of the promising young men in the field of cricket, being a useful all-rounder. I was generally expected to make a modest contribution with the bat, and to the taking of wickets as an off-break bowler. My presence at first or second slip, on the other hand, often gave great credit to our fast bowlers.

For several years our Club had been actively engaged in second-class Cricket Competitions and, having attained its peak, had now been promoted to the first class division. With great excitement and delight, we were determined to prove ourselves worthy of the new status by our performance in the first class Cricket Competition. It was ruñ by the most reputable cricketing body in San Fernando, the second largest town on the island, about four miles from our village. Many of our matches were played in what was known as Paradise Pasture, later Skinner Park, and I recall up to this day some of the remarkable events and highlights of that first match.

After considerable excitement amongst the players and supporters of both sides, the match ended in a close draw. I had made a useful contribution, but our captain at the time was the main contributor. He was destructive with the bat as well as with the ball. His medium pace, off-break bowling was of great merit. But the most spectacular feat of the occasion was the dismissal of the best batsman of the opposing team. He had struck a ball forcefully high into the air towards the long-on boundary where our captain was deployed.

The ball had crashed among the branches of a tall tree near the boundary line, and ricocheted from one branch to another with a rapidity of deflection that taxed our captain's reflexes to the full. Darting about – changing course – in pursuit of the ball, he somehow managed to retain his useful composure with his green-peeked cap pulled down over his brows. In making the catch, he stumbled and fell to the ground, rolling over twice, but the hand with the ball was held, raised high for all to see. A tremendous applause erupted simultaneously, and our seal as a formidable contender in the competition was firmly set.

During further encounters in the cricket field, our outstanding fast bowler, one of my younger brothers, himself a formidable medium fast bowler with a good length out-swinger, always maintained their position at the top of our attacking force, in addition to our captain and myself.

We had as wicket-keepers, a tall Negro of six feet four inches and, in contrast, a short Indian, no taller than five feet. They were both very good keepers. A good team-spirit was one of our greatest attributes, from which we derived a great deal of pleasure and gave to others likewise.

Our Captain was one of the best sportsmen I ever knew. Apart from his prowess on the cricket field, he was a great athlete. I did not realise that at the time, as I was about four years his junior. He was also a clever boxer, wrestler, runner and swimmer. He, our fast bowler and I, as young men frequently went for a three-mile run at about 5 o'clock nearly every morning, then on to the hot springs before going out to work. We all worked with the Oil Refining Company. Our captain was engaged in a Refining Plant as far as I can remember, while our fast bowler was engaged in clerical work at one of the field offices in which I was engaged as an engineering draughtsman during the early stages of our career.

Paul, our renowned fast bowler, was much nearer my age, and as such we spent a lot of time together, especially during the period of school leaving age, while waiting for suitable employment. I never knew how we found so much time to roam through the sugar-cane fields, the woods and forests, seeking out our favourite mango trees, bird watching, crab catching, and to indulge in sea-bathing – swimming often twice a day.

Reverting to the subject of cricket, I refer to the delight and joy we, as poor country folks, experienced seated on bench forms on an open lorry, heading into town as first-class cricketers. We did well to have commanded great respect, and although we had not succeeded in winning the Cup, we had gained a great deal of experience and helped to put our village club in the limelight for quite some time. And gone were the days when local battles for supremacy in the second-class division took us and our supporters into remote villages to contest the issues with some very cantankerous opposition.

I recall an instance in which the captain of the opposing side had spun a coin to decide the winner of the toss. It was the third time that we were matched against that particular club on their home ground, and on each occasion, had lost the toss. One of our eagle-eyed supporters spotted the two-headed coin, quickly retrieved by the captain of the other side who had spun it. There was an emphatic denial, but he refused to exhibit the coin for inspection. During the process of a prolonged heated argument, a screeching voice, well above all others, cried out: 'Thief, thief! Bloody thief!' and jeered with prolonged mocking laughter.

We were three miles from home, on foreign territory. All our members and supporters looked round with concern and trepidation, for the villagers in that area were reputed to be stick fighters of a quarrelsome nature. The screeching voice repeated its accusation. The captain of the home team suddenly leapt into the air, reeling off expressions in Hindustani. He was finally restrained by members of his team. But the trouble-maker, a talkative parrot of one of the two feuding families in the area, began to inflame the situation all over again, uttering the most vile and corrupt swear words in Hindustani, punctuated by raucous screeching and jeering, non-stop.

There was no restraining this time, and so we hurriedly departed, under protest, as the two families were at each other's throats with parrots from each side joining in with vile and vociferous remarks.

It was their desperate dash for their weapons of war – sticks, cutlass and catapult – that hastened out immediate retreat. Both families and their jeering parrots were still being heard quite some distance away.

29

Moonlight Excursion: Twin-sisters

I had always taken an active part in the running of the village Cricket Club, and on diverse occasions had been on the Committee and had held the post of captain from time to time. At one stage I was principally concerned with the raising of funds necessary to meet the regular expenditure. The major fund-raising enterprise has been a well-organised public dance, held annually at Claxton Bay, about three miles away.

On occasions, moonlight excursions to selected beaches not only proved profitable, but fired and maintained the interest of all our members and supporters. As leader of the village band, I was well placed to take on this responsibility of arranging for the music. On a particular occasion, I organised a moonlight bus excursion to one of the popular beaches on the south coast of the island and arrangements were made for dancing on the beach, to the strains of our village band, with myself as leader. It was a great attraction, and was well attended.

Being the principal organiser, I distributed the responsibility equally among the Committee Members, and took on a supervisory role, in addition to looking after the rendition of suitable pieces of music during the journey, and on the beach.

Although I was kept well occupied in the circumstances, I found time for a dip into the warm sea and had a few leisurely strokes in the water. To me, it was a peaceful way of handling the situation and maintaining quiet surveillance of the proceedings at the same time. While walking along the beach, a young woman seated on the sand at the water margin seemed to be in great discomfort as she anxiously rubbed her legs, gasping somewhat.

'What's the matter?' I enquired.

'I think it's cramp,' she replied.

I was no stranger to such complaints. I had my first-aid kit in the bus with some liniment for that purpose.

'I'll bring some medicine for you; wait a moment!' I said, as I hurried off to the bus for the kit.

On my way back I met her coming towards me, being assisted by another young woman very much like herself, but without a limp. We were now nearer to the bus in which the first aid kit was kept than where I'd left her, so they came over with me to the bus. They introduced themselves as Doreen and Maureen and I saw for the first time in my life identical twin-sisters. I was astounded, but I kept my secret. It was Doreen who complained of cramp. I handed the liniment to her but she passed it back and asked me to rub it on for her if I didn't mind.

I had applied the ointment to my own legs and to those of other men during our long sessions of sea bathing, but I had never applied it before to a girl's ankle, let alone the upper regions of her thighs. I went about the task with some trepidation but in a most professional manner, for the study of medicine had long been in the back of my mind.

Doreen began whimpering in an extraordinary manner. Believing that I was doing more harm than good, I stopped abruptly and asked her if it was all right.

She replied, 'Yes, it's very good – it's lovely.'

Immediately, her sister asked for both her legs to be rubbed also, as she smiled a winsome smile.

The sisters were dressed alike, in a red close-fitting swim-suit, it was very difficult to tell them apart. However, by the application of the ointment, Maureen appeared to be the bolder and more excitable.

The excursion was successful in terms of a quiet and satisfying venture. The financial gain was always a secondary matter in such cases for it was generally looked upon as a treat for the Club Members and supporters. It was also an advertisement for the Club in advance to our grand annual dance.

I had heard of the twin-sisters, but never had I imagined that they could be so much alike. Having been caught up in that predicament, I found it difficult to ignore the rousing curiosity which had begun to beset me, but I kept myself in check despite reflections of the recent Carnival Dance and City Carnival.

About two months later I received an invitation from the twin-sisters to play with my band on the occasion of their birthday celebration at their home, and offered to provide the necessary transport both ways. I was surprised, and very delighted; but beneath this delight, was my apprehension of being carried away by those two charming and beautiful girls. The members of the band were in full accord and, on the Saturday evening in question, with transport provided, we were taken to their home. We comprised a quartet, quite appropriate for the occasion.

All members of the band were employed by the Oil Company, and saw one another nearly every day. The bass player was of Spanish/Portuguese descent. He was an amicable middle-aged man who put his whole heart into the playing of his instrument, so much so that he was often left playing alone at the end of a piece of music. He spoke Spanish fluently, and was a very kind man. He was a pipe fitter by trade. The banjo player was a first-class welder with the firm. He had a good command of his instrument – tenor banjo – and delighted enthusiasts by effective use of the entire length of the finger board.

Philip, the saxophonist, was the only reader of sheet music in the band. As such, he was regarded as a man of knowledge. Indeed he was better educated than any other member of the band, myself included, but it made no difference whatsoever among us. Despite his knowledge of music, however, or because of it, he was strongly advised to keep his sight on his sheet, because he couldn't sing in tune. His playing, therefore, ran amok if his eyes were not glued to the sheet. He produced a beautiful sleepy tune on his instrument, and occasionally played himself to sleep in the process, especially if he had a trying day at his work. He was an Accountant's Clerk. Like the bass player, he was of Spanish/Portuguese decent and like myself, the banjo player was of Negro stock, but neither of these differences mattered in the least.

I am certain that there were many peculiarities about my clarinet playing as well but on the whole, we were a merry band, and that's what really mattered.

My heavy commitment in the pursuit of correspondence courses connected with my work had ruled out the idea of frequent rehearsals of the band. I simply decided on the most suitable calypso tunes and learned them off by ear. After deciding on the keys in which they should be played, I passed the word on to the players, each of whom was accustomed to playing anything on the spur of the moment, except for the saxophonist who was obliged to have the music before him.

The birthday celebration of the twin-sisters was a very enjoyable affair with only a few guests, even though they lived in a large house all to themselves. During the course of the evening it came to light that the house was their ancestral home on their mother's side, also with a history of identical twins in their family.

The house was their mutual inheritance and, in addition, they were celebrating the third anniversary of their partnership for they became joint owners of the property on their twenty-first birthday. Pleased to be only twenty-four and the sole occupants of the house, they considered themselves fortunate. They were of mixed blood, their father being African descent and mother a Spaniard. They had taken mainly after their mother. Their auburn, long and curly hair hung limply about their necks and shapely shoulders. Despite their rather slim physique, there was an amazing feminine fullness about them both, no doubt accentuated by their habitual attention to physical exercises. They were both teachers in a country school not far from their home in the country. Their mother died when they were seventeen, and their father was employed as an Engineer with an Oil Drilling company in Venezuela, South America.

There was no distinction between members of the band and any of the guests present. We were all treated alike, even though it was obvious that a few of their relations and friends were in attendance. The whole affair took the form of a party, or rather, a small gathering of close acquaintances of which all members of the band were privileged guests. And so with two dozen or more people in attendance, there was little music-playing and lots of chatter and refreshments. Lighthearted and carefree conversation were the order of the occasion – a very enjoyable and enlightening one it was indeed.

On leaving their house late that evening, the sisters stood one at each side of the open door to see us off, shaking hands as we parted. My palm closed instinctively on saying goodnight and had not released its firm clench until I had entered the privacy of my own bedroom that night.

Carefully opening my hand, I found a squashed bit of

paper – note paper – inviting me to have tea with them at four o'clock the following Sunday afternoon. I did not know which one of the twins had written the note. It ended thus: 'With best wishes from D and M.'

I was in a quandary, for I had not bargained for anything of the sort. I knew that both sisters were curious about me, as I was about them I suppose, but I did not know on what account. It certainly was not because of their interest in music, otherwise they would have suggested that I play a piece of music for them to accompany. They both played the piano to the extent that they held private classes at their home. Their maturity and general knowledge gave me a feeling of inferiority and my first inclination was to back away from it all. But yet again, there was that nagging curiosity, far from being quelled, and it must have shone through to both girls.

I felt that I wanted to know more and more about them in just the same way I wanted to know about the cravat (my favourite wild bird) my work, clarinet . . . but there was something puzzling about them apart from their being identical. Above all, I wanted to be able to simply identify one from the other.

In the process of my deliberation, my reply had been delayed to the extent that it had become too late to refuse without being discourteous. Therefore, I cycled over to their home one evening at dusk and delivered my reply through their letter-box, accepting an invitation.

One of the considerations that helped in arriving at the decision to accept was the prospect of a job in Venezuela for which I understood the rate was three or four times the salary I was being paid. I would find out the name and address of the Oil Company with which their father was employed, I thought, or that he would put me onto something. Those were some of my considerations, because I knew that I was grossly underpaid, and had little or no prospects of improvement with my employers in the foreseeable future.

At 4 o'clock on the Sunday afternoon, I knocked on their front door and was pleasantly welcomed by one of the sisters. I couldn't tell which one she was, and I fervently hoped that they would not be dressed alike. Just as I was about to ask about her sister, I was told that Maureen would soon be with us. I knew then, that I was in the company of Doreen, who, it was disclosed at the birthday party, was the elder. I recalled that it was Doreen who had complained of cramp on the beach in the first place, on the evening of the moonlight excursion.

Immediately, Maureen joined us in their sitting room and greeted: 'Hello, you must excuse me for not being at the door to greet you.'

Oh, that's quite all right. Doreen explained that you would be here soon,' I replied.

'Yes, I did ask him to excuse you,' confirmed Doreen.

The voice sounded just as though Maureen had spoken again, for the intonation and manner of speech were very similar. Both girls were dressed alike, in a pale blue frilly dress, open neck and back with hem just below the knees. Suspecting my uneasiness about their likeness, Doreen quickly pointed out that she was wearing a wrist watch.

After some light conversation, we retreated to the dining-room. It was Maureen who had prepared the tea, and very delightful it was, but we were all light eaters, so very little was consumed.

Foremost in my mind was the matter of boosting my salary by obtaining employment abroad, for quite a few of my colleagues had done so. But I wanted to go to Venezuela legally, not by underground methods and be caught and tortured. Furthermore, I had no intention of breaking the law.

Thus on returning to the sitting-room I asked, 'By the way, have you a map of Venezuela handy?'

I didn't direct my question to anyone in particular for fear of being misunderstood.

'Oh yes, but mainly of the region where Daddy is working,' one of them replied enthusiastically, I didn't know which one. Both were delighted in the interest I appeared to have taken.

'Maureen, fetch the two maps from the bookcase, I'll bring the folding table from the kitchen, and let's show Jacob the region where Daddy's working,' Doreen remarked eagerly.

'Good, that's a good idea, I'm very interested,' I said.

'Why, do you want to work in Venezuela, then?'

'Oh, I'm very interested,' I replied.

Our attention has now focused on a large small-scale map and a tiny spot apparently in the middle of nowhere.

Seated on the couch with each sister one on each side eagerly cuddling up to me, was awkward enough, but the jostling of hands and fingers, criss-crossing over a tiny spot on the map quickly deflected waning enthusiasm to the pursuit of a more immediate enterprise. There was a mounting emotional fervour, and I knew that it was time for me to make my departure.

It may have seemed a little ill-mannered to leave somewhat abruptly, but the pressure of coping with my correspondence courses was appreciated and accepted as a valid excuse. But I was urged to let up a bit and don't forget that 'Too much work and no play. . . .' I knew exactly what they meant. At least I thought they meant that I must devote more time to leisure. This was confirmed when they suggested that I spend longer time with them on my next occasion. I thanked them kindly and they saw me off.

214

30

Grenada Holiday

In my endeavour to raise funds for our village cricket club, bus excursions to various beaches all over the island were organised from time to time. On this account, I had seen most of our seashores and had frequently visited the many beautiful sites. Even so there seemed to be a lasting beauty that prompted a re-visit to certain areas. But with advancing age and maturity, I began to focus my attention to the neighbouring islands. And so it was a matter of course that in 1936, I went on an excursion to the island of Grenada by ship. It was the first time that I had set foot beyond the shores of my homeland.

Like most islands in the West Indies, Grenada was very beautiful, and particularly impressive were the white sands stretched along the captivating Grand Anse beach. The coastline in the region extended as far as I was able to see, fringed with lush greenery. The placid blue waters gently lapping her shores more than stretched my imagination. Trinidad was generally looked upon as an island of great opportunities because of its mineral resources, but Grenada and the other Caribbean Islands have their outstanding characteristic virtues.

During the afternoon on the day following our arrival at St George's, the capital, Arthur Lucas and I went to the famous Grand Anse beach for some relaxation. We were both struck by its hypnotic beauty, even though we had heard of it before setting off on the excursion.

Arthur and I became acquainted while on the ship for the first time. He, too, was born in Trinidad. While basking leisurely in a quiet region, in shallow waters, we saw two figures in the distance, swimming towards us. They stopped at about 100 feet from us, and we slowly advanced towards them to make enquiries and to learn about the local places of interest. We soon discovered that they were two young women.

Arthur, very eager to make the acquaintance, called out, 'Hello!'

There was an enthusiastic response and a casual conversation ensued.

Arthur was a little taller and less sturdy than I, of average height. He was handsome and well-built, very quick to make new acquaintances and, similarly, very quick to end them, not being ever popular in his choice in the first place, as far as I gathered from his account of events during our conversations and my brief observations. Like myself, he was a black man.

Ethel, the taller of the two young women (or girls, as they were called in such instances), seemed to be of a temperament matching Arthur's. Thus within moments they swam off to a 'basking ground' of their own, after having made some informal introduction.

Edna remained with me, and casually we talked about matters of general interest. She was a very attractive girl, quiet and well-spoken. Her brown skin possessed a sheen, typical of good health, and her movements, both beneath and on the surface of the water, were delightful to watch.

Ethel and Arthur, meanwhile, seemed to be in close harmony with lots of chatter and laughter, energetically threshing the water about them. Edna was momentarily lost as she gazed in their direction, no doubt sportingly envious of her friend's indulgence. But somehow, such

216

frolics tended to invoke memories which made me shy away from the occasion of close encounter with girls, until I knew more about the strange feelings I experienced in similar instances in the past. Now we were about to rejoin forces, with Ethel leading the way back to our original basking ground, as it were. I suspected a coolness in the relationship between Arthur and Ethel on their return.

Ethel and Edna seemed delighted to be together once more, and before returning to their original meeting place, Arthur and I were reminded about a popular dance in town later that evening.

I was very keen to meet the musicians, and to listen to their music. Therefore, I arrived at the dance hall before their arrival. I made an acquaintance with the band leader and was invited to accompany them to the stage after introducing myself as a clarinettist from Trinidad. They made me feel completely at ease. Although I chatted with all the members of the six-piece band, my main attention was directed to the clarinettist for the obvious reason of having a common interest. With the tuning of the instruments accomplished, the band struck up in lively mood and the dancers fanned out across the floor of the dance hall.

Because of the expectant crowd, the musicians provided me with a seat on the stage which was reserved for them, and it was from that vantage point that I saw the entry of Ethel and Edna, unescorted, to the hall. But, no sooner had they entered than they were virtually swept away by watchful discerning eyes, for they were both conspicuously radiant. Ethel, in a light-yellow dress with deep blue under-garment that asserted itself through the semi-transparency of the dress. While, in complementary colours, the ribbon in her hair, her earrings, necklace, bracelets and shoes – all – gave credence to her exquisite taste. Her dark, smooth skin, glistening with health, seemed to draw attention to characteristics of her person which, only much later, I understood to be but a fraction of the seductive features of the human female. She seemed totally different from the Ethel who, with her friend Edna, had joined Arthur and me on the beach earlier that afternoon. I had hardly noticed her then, but here, from the stage in the dance hall, as she danced by, I saw the beautiful shape of her mouth, the fullness of her attractive lips, her eyes, brows and her smile . . . all those things seemed totally at variance with the impression I had at our first encounter, while basking in the sun only a few hours ago. How strange, I thought. My eyes must have been half closed at the time.

Arthur arrived on the scene somewhat later, and came over to the band to say hello. Within a few minutes he took to the floor. He danced with Ethel for a while, but the competition for her hand was such that showed him to be an unfortunate contender. He then sought anyone at random.

Eventually, he pursued Edna's company and spent most of the time dancing with her. I made a point of dancing with her on a few occasions earlier.

Feeling now that I ought to approach Ethel, I eventually took the bold step, knowing that my dancing was of a poor standard. In order to avoid disappointment, I made my request to her beforehand. She was delightfully agreeable. The band struck up. It was a slow foxtrot. Before I knew what was happening, Ethel and I were on the floor moving along with the flowing tide of dancers.

'Oh, so sorry,' I apologised. 'I did tell you that I was no good at dancing, Ethel . . . remember?' I remarked softly.

'Don't you worry one bit; you're doing well. Let's carry on.'

'But you are so good. Did you attend classes?' I asked.

'Yes, when I was at college most of the girls went to

private classes, so I finally decided to take lessons as well so as not to appear too much of an oddity.'

'Well, I must say, you did very well indeed.'

'I wouldn't say so really, but thank you just the same,' she responded, smiling gently in appreciation of my observations, as we danced.

Now the music suddenly changed to a quickstep to which neither of us was inclined so we decided to sit it out with some refreshments. As we engaged ourselves in light conversation, I discovered that Ethel was a teacher in biology at a village school in the district where she was born.

While still in conversation with Ethel, reviewing some of her remarks, I said, 'Tell me, Ethel, being a teacher at a school in your native district, you must be a very popular person there, or at least, very well-known.'

'Well, that sort of thing has a lot of setbacks. For one thing, I grew up under the strict discipline of my grandmother and have hardly been out of the place at all. And I'm twenty-seven, fancy that. I feel that I'm my own woman now and I intend to make the best of the next few days I have here, in town. What about you? What is your work?' she enquired with a deep sense of interest.

'I'm an engineering draughtsman, involved in mechanical and structural work mainly, but some reinforced concrete construction and some surveying are frequently thrown in,' I said casually.

'My word, my word! That sounds rather technical.'

'I dare say it does, and the type of drawing bears the name "technical", but I suppose it's no more difficult than the study of biology,' I asserted, smiling.

We both smiled for we enjoyed a very refreshing conversation.

Although one of my uncles and two of my brothers were school teachers, I had no idea what biology was about at that time, and I felt ashamed to show up my ignorance. Yet I had a compelling urge to ask her about it, fearing that I would feel even more ashamed to ask someone whom I knew better.

Thus, at a convenient moment, I broached her on the subject. She hesitated, a little surprised I suppose, then smiling, said that it deals with 'The facts of life'. There was an uneasy silence for a few moments, for my impression, so far, was that the facts of life were the elements such as the sun and the rain, night and day, and the existence of the moon and the stars and matters of that nature. She had seen my predicament.

'How old are you, by the way?' she asked.

I told her that I was twenty-five. There was another period of silence. Thoughts of the twin sisters had entered my mind. 'Did I offend you?' she asked searchingly, almost in a whisper, as she leaned her head towards me.

'Oh no, no, not at all. I was just thinking. . . .'

'I was thinking too,' she interrupted. 'When is your boat leaving?' she continued.

When I told her that it would be leaving in two days' time, she said that she would really like to discuss more about 'The facts of life' because it was very important that one should know what it really means, and what it is all about.

The interval was over and the music had resumed with great gusto. Ethel was in such demand that it would have been too embarrassing to engage her attention any longer at that moment, but later on we danced again for quite a while, and arranged to meet when the dance was over, or the following day.

Arthur and Edna were in close company, so to speak, and had disappeared long before the dance was over. I remained until the end.

On leaving the stage after saying goodbye to the

musicians, I saw two men talking to Ethel. She had glanced back a few times, and I assumed that she may have been waiting to say goodnight to me. As I approached her, she stretched out her hands; I received them warmly, and her companions withdrew. I accompanied her to the front door of her hotel, and we confirmed arrangements for the following day.

A beautiful moon, set high in the sky, had cast a brilliant lustre over the island, with a hallowing charm. I felt uplifted in a way that could not really be explained. It was as though I was being blessed by the Heavens for the manner of my conduct.

Ethel and I met later in the day, for it was already in the early hours of the morning when we parted. We visited several places of interest in and outside the capital, and spent some enjoyable moments lazing in the beautiful waters, and on the sands at Grand Anse. During that period, we had developed a sympathetic relationship in which caring for the well-being of each other and the whole of humanity had been our main purpose oblivious of all other matters. She had engaged my deepest thoughts.

Some time later, she explained that she was awarded a grant and intended leaving for England in three months' time for a degree in biology, and suggested that it would be a good idea for me to learn more about 'The facts of life', she said, shyly and somewhat pensively. She added, 'An elder girl would be best.' It was time for us to depart, and she abruptly said goodbye, kissed me on the cheek and walked away, leaving me puzzled by the statement: 'An elder girl. . . .'

I stood and watched her disappear in the distance, feeling that I had lost a close friend. The excursion ship returned to Port-of-Spain safely and I was soon back home and at work dealing with the backlog which had accumulated during my absence. And that applied equally in respect of my work with the firm, and my correspondence courses.

31

Jury Service

I settled quickly to my usual pattern of work with my colleagues in the Drawing Office. They all showed a lively interest in the various aspects of my holiday.

'Well, did you have a nice time?' Alex enquired.

He was one of the most pleasant kind-hearted men I'd ever known and had been engaged with the firm for over four years. He knew it was my first trip abroad, and in fact, had encouraged me to go on the excursion. Being about twenty years my senior, and a draughtsman of considerable experience, he had taught me a great deal and was very helpful to me. His primary interests in my holiday were about the various resorts, the architecture, contour of the land and the industrial outlook. He was happily married. I admired him and was grateful for his guidance. The couple had had no offspring.

He then came to the nature of the people and, surprisingly, he asked whether I had made some friends, with girls in particular.

Alex was of light-brown complexion and curly greying hair. He had travelled widely, including visits to the United States, England, Germany, India and Australia. Not the Alex I knew as a child. He once said to me in confidence, that my work was far in advance of his, and that it was unfair that he should be paid so much and I so little in terms of salary. He was indeed the most broad-minded man I had ever known. Hence, when he mentioned the matter of girl friends, although I was caught by surprise, I was certain that he had my interests at heart.

Thus, in answer to his enquiry, I told him what my observations were, and also about my transient relationship with Ethel. He explained that for quite some time he thought that I should be mixing more closely with members of the opposite sex, and that while caution is necessary, if my isolation from them was taken too far, a strange unhealthy complex could develop in time. He suggested that Ethel was unusual in that she was very sensitive, sympathetic and sincere; and he agreed to a great extent with what she had said. My problem was then to find out what aspect of Ethel's observation he was in disagreement with, but I dared not take the matter further. I needed time to think. Shortly after that conversation with Alex, I was summoned to Jury Service.

Many interesting cases had been brought for trial, some of which comprised attempted murder, manslaughter, arson and rape. I followed the arguments closely and believed that I made a worthwhile contribution to the general cause. During the recess and at other intervals, several related and unrelated cases were discussed in private among the members of the Jury. Most of the incidents were quite comical and put some light-heartedness in the whole sordid affair.

One of the members who had topped the score in relating such incidents told us about a case in which a man and woman were frequently appearing before the courts, charged with assault or causing grievous bodily harm or disturbing the peace – often a case of multiple charges. On this occasion, the man had overstepped the mark, and the injury to the woman gave cause for great concern. The man was sentenced to go to prison for six months. The woman thereupon protested strongly, she became hysterical and fainted, but soon recovered. After consultation among the lawyers, it was disclosed that although the couple were not married, he was the father of their five children and was the sole supporter of their young family. This called for an urgent muffled discussion at the bench, after which the woman was asked if she had anything to say why sentence to prison should not be passed.

Now fully recovered from her sobbing, she replied, 'All I want to know is who gonna give me the money to feed me five children if day farther is lock up in gaol . . . done bother bout me, but dee chillrun muss heat,' she concluded.

There was another meeting of legal heads, in a desperate attempt to solve the predicament.

Because facilities were more favourable for married couples, the question was put to her, 'Why don't you get married?'

Immediately came the answer, 'Because I don't love him. I never did and I never will.'

Having objected to all compromises put to her, she was threatened with imprisonment for a fortnight.

Another case had taken an almost similar line. A man had run up a considerable debt by purchasing goods from a woman with whom he had become very familiar, because of her grocery shop. After several fruitless demands for her money, she took the matter to court. The defendant was found to be a penniless scoundrel, and was sentenced to serve three months in gaol. Here, too, the woman was very disappointed and angry. In her protestation, she demanded the money owing to her for goods she had sold to the defendant.

Despite the Court's order to be quiet, she kept up a continuous wailing, 'I don't want no locking up, I want me money! You hear?'

Her continuous repetition had so antagonized the Court that she was finally charged with contempt and ordered to pay a fine of fifty dollars, or go to prison for ten days.

Many of these 'back room' cases related by a few members of the Jury, off duty as it were, were incidents which may have occurred at the lower courts somewhere or another in the country, or even fabricated. From all the chatter, however, came some valuable information and presented views of the world I'd seen for the first time. Many aspects, even though indirectly, certainly helped in the maturity of my judgment.

Let me mention another account of a case of over-indulgence, as related by another colleague, again during our off-duty period.

An enthusiastic young policeman, convinced that his way to the top depended upon the number of successful prosecutions accounted on his behalf, he prompted some of his relatives to commit some petty crimes, and he would settle the matter. He had suggested to them the nature of the crime, and engineered their arrest, which he himself carried out, with the understanding that he would pay any fines incurred.

He had made considerable progress, but wishing to make even greater strides, by a similar arrangement, he arrested his own mother. This unusual incident created a stir in his rural village, and people from all around flooded the court room to listen to the hearing.

The young constable with his eye on three stripes, held his head up high, as he watched his mother approach the dock. But, the nature of her crime warranted a prison sentence, and his mother was sent to gaol for three months. His mother wept bitterly. The police officer suffered a severe nervous breakdown and was eventually discharged from the Force, on grounds of ill health. There seemed no end to such incidents. One only hoped that justice was being done, and that it will always be done.

32

Twin-Sisters Revisited

During the period of my Jury Service, I had taken part in discussions with several of my colleagues, most of whom were much older than I. I had gained a great deal of confidence and felt much more capable of holding an intelligent conversation with the twin-sisters, or with anyone else for that matter, on issues of everyday life.

Grand thoughts of the sisters had been on my mind a great deal, somehow, so I decided that, at twenty-five, I must assert myself, although I didn't know in what way I should do so. They did not always dress alike, but when they did, I was thrown into a peculiar state of uneasiness, but, decided to deal with that when the situation arose.

Judging from my conversation with Ethel, the biology teacher I met during my holiday in Grenada, it seemed a good opportunity to broach the delicate matter of 'The facts of life' as she had suggested. And what seemed very strange was that I did not want them to have the occasion of discussing it with anyone else. I disliked feeling the way I did, because it seemed so selfish. But, I concluded that if no harm was committed, then there was nothing wrong in feeling the way I did.

I waited until the Club Dance was staged. The sisters attended in dazzling raiment as usual, and had assisted in promoting it. It was a great success, and I took the opportunity of introducing them to Mr Toma, the president of the Cricket Club.

Mr Toma was a widely-travelled, middle-aged man with greying hair, tall, well-mannered with a pleasant personality. Doreen and her sister had heard quite a lot about him in very favourable terms, and were delighted to make the personal acquaintance. Although it was not really necessary, I thought the new acquaintanceship would endear the sisters to me, and in that way, they would become ardent supporters of the Cricket Club.

The following day, during a discussion in respect of the proceeds of the dance, Mr Toma made a casual reference to the twin-sisters. Complimentary though it was I experienced a fleeting disquiet. He remarked that they were impressively identical and were delightfully charming. Mr Toma being a man of knowledge, I was pleased to note his observations.

Now, I had a greater desire than ever to discover what physical differences there were between them, because of my confusion in not being able to distinguish one from the other. The thought of it made me nervous and a bit weary; thus I decided to make some casual observations only without appearing to be rude or unethical.

Despite the impelling nature of my curiosity, the real driving force in the whole affair was my fervent desire to secure employment with an oil company in Venezuela, South America. It was rumoured that high wages were paid there; as an engineering draughtsman and surveyor, I felt that I would be well-placed.

The father of the twin-sisters was employed with an engineering firm there at the time, and I believed that my friendship with them would enable me to obtain some valuable information from their father. Thus I warmly entertained the idea of becoming closely acquainted with the twins.

At the height of my romantic notions, I received an

invitation from the sisters to have tea with them one Sunday evening. It was shortly after our Cricket Club Dance, and the handwritten note was signed by them both, so it seemed. I was very excited and replied in the affirmative, even though I viewed the occasion with some anxiety.

At the appointed time, I called at the house and both sisters this time, came to answer my call at the front door. Their identical smiles welcomed me and at once I was made to feel at home. Immediately, they identified themselves, for they could easily have made a fool of anyone if they wished, but they never did such things as far as I was aware.

It was the height of the dry season, and they sported a very short flared white dress with blue dots, sleeveless with a low cut at the top – front and back. As they walked across the room daintily, half glancing back, their images reflecting on the highly polished floor seemed like imaginary dolls in a fairy tale, and the fact that they were identical added great interest and excitement, and an air of mysticism to the occasion.

We entered the sitting-room and sat on a couch where we indulged in lighthearted conversations relating to the Club Dance.

'Look here, before we go any further I want to thank both of you on behalf of the committee for your valuable assistance at the club dance,' I remarked, but this was soon pushed aside.

They wanted to know all about my stay in Grenada, this gave me the opportunity I wanted. I explained all I could about the beach and other beauty spots on the island, but their main concern was about people. They were pretty, vain, and, in particular, they wanted to know if I had met good-looking pretty girls. This gave me the opportunity to refer to Ethel who, from all accounts, was much more involved with the subject of biology than were the sisters. And when my ignorance of 'The facts of life' had surfaced, they were not able to conceal the puckish gleam in their eyes. I was now assailed by a barrage of flirtatious postures. Without restraint, Maureen, the younger sister, hurried over to a cabinet in a corner of the room, and set in play a gramophone record with exotic Latin American music such as I had played at the celebration dance for the Carnival King and Queen at San Fernando only a few years ago.

'No, Maureen, no!' her sister exclaimed in an attempt to subdue her passion, but she was already on the floor, dancing to the music, in the image of a Carnival Queen, steeped in sensuality.

In order not to be outdone, Doreen joined in the frolic and together they exhibited a complex combination of convulsive posturing, surpassing all that I'd ever seen. As soon as the music on the side of the record had ended, Doreen quickly set off another record – her favourite. The much slower tempo brought to light further startling revelation, in slow motion, by contrast. The sisters also displayed on a combination of ballet and gymnastic configurations, gracefully interwoven with a series of spontaneous and identical flowing movements. At times they approached each other, one from the left, the other from the right, and converging in the middle, they appeared to slide through each other. They appeared as a single individual at the mid-point, seemed to emerge on opposite sides.

'There is something uncanny, but how could there be? They are real,' I told myself.

It seemed as though a strange world had loomed into existence. A world far in advance of my time; a world that would swallow me up, were I not to heed the deeper promptings of my mind.

231

I was seated in the middle portion of the couch and as soon as the music stopped, they glided over and sat one at each side of me, chuckling, slightly out of breath with sparkling eyes looking deep into mine. I felt afraid.

'Well, did you like our dance?' they asked, both at the same time.

They glanced at each other, then looked at me again. The manner of their dance, and even the atmosphere, seemed so unreal . . . as though we were in a different world. I was momentarily overwhelmed.

'Would you like to try?' Doreen asked.

'Yes, how about that, won't you like to?' Maureen added in support of her sister as she sprang up from her seat with outstretched hands directed towards me.

'No! It was I who suggested it. Let me teach you,' said Doreen, beckoning Maureen out of the way, both still breathing heavily after their energetic display.

Politely declining the offer, I explained that I was not a dancer by any means, and that playing the clarinet for others to dance, prevented me from learning.

'Well, this is just the time to make a start,' Doreen said.

'Go on,' insisted Maureen. 'Oh, I know, he's shy,' she added.

'No, he's not,' said Doreen.

'Yes he is.'

'No he isn't.'

Well, let's ask him then,' both sisters remarked at the same time.

They looked at each other again and smiled. I joined in the smile without commitment. However, my promise to take dancing lessons at some time in the future was warmly appreciated. My anxiety was thus allayed.

'I think I'll have a quick bath right away,' said Doreen, briskly.

'I too,' said Maureen, then said to me, 'You can come

and give us a hand if you wish,' as she glided along the passage to the bathroom. Having been given the freedom of the house earlier on, I elected to put on an old classical record.

Within moments, there was an urgent call, 'Jacob, it's Maureen, please could you give me a brisk rub? Hurry, I'm getting cold.'

I felt very nervous and vulnerable a while ago, but suddenly it seemed as though some particular aspect of my being had taken over. And I felt all the better for it. I hurried along the passage in response to Maureen's call, with a strictly clinical approach.

The bedroom door was left ajar, and as I advanced towards it, she called out, 'In here, come in.'

On entering the room, I faltered, not knowing what to expect.

'Don't be shy, I'm not,' she remarked in way of boosting my confidence.

Lying face downwards on the bed, partly wrapped in a bath towel, she asserted, 'It's my back that needs a brisk rubbing, I've done my front already,' she glanced up while handing me the towel, smiling.

By adopting a professional approach, in a clinical manner, I had held Maureen's exuberance in check. Lamont's timely intervention had finally brought her seductive posturing to an end. My purpose at this stage had been completed. I sensed that my protector had interceded on my behalf.

I left the sisters in the bedroom which they shared, each on her own bed. While awaiting their return to the sitting-room, I pondered the prospects of being able to maintain such a relationship and, indeed, whether or not it would be in my interest. In those silent moments, it became clear that if my solemn objectives were to be achieved, I should make my departure as soon as possible, without appearing to be discourteous.

There was not a sound anywhere in the house. The urge to leave had become overpowering. I was in great conflict within myself, then suddenly I reached for pencil and paper in my trousers pocket, wrote a polite note of appreciation, thanked them and asked to be excused for my abrupt departure. I promised to keep in touch with them but had no idea when and how, or if ever. . . .

33

Tobago Holiday

Excursions to our neighbouring islands by ship had been on the increase following my visit to Grenada in 1936 and now, three years later, I decided it was time that I should visit our sister island, Tobago. As soon as I boarded the ship I fell into conversation with a Mr Morello, the overseer of an old-fashioned, run-down estate. He was a middle-aged, heavily built black man, affable and well-mannered. In the course of our conversation, he told me that he was returning home from a well-spent and very enjoyable holiday in Trinidad. He had been a widower for only three months and had not yet adapted to his new mode of life.

Having explained that I was on my first visit to Tobago, he invited me to stay at his home if I wished, and that he could take me to the farm on a hunt if I cared for that kind of sport.

'By the way,' he said, 'Just call me George.'

We travelled by the same coastal ship as I did on the occasion of my visit to Grenada. In like manner, the voyage was excellent. His friend Luther was at the quay to meet him, and gave him an enthusiastic welcome. I was introduced to him immediately and was warmly received.

Luther was also a black man, tall, large and loud speaking, full of life. Well-meaning, he took up the matter of my lodgings. Mr Morello offered me accommodation, which I accepted on the understanding that I would be happier to pay a charge.

Immediately we arrived at George's home, I was shown around the house, and taken to the room given to me. Through a large window on one side there was an exciting view of the sea, and from another window part of the farm was clearly visible. It was late afternoon and I decided to spend the rest of the day sorting out my affairs and acquainting myself with the geography of the Island. A visit to the town and to one of the popular beaches was arranged for the following day, and the day after that would be a grand-event – the hunt.

On the visit to the town and to the beach, we were joined by other members from Trinidad and a few of George's and Luther's friends. It was Sunday afternoon and despite the number of people about, it was rather surprising that more had not taken to the beach in such glorious weather.

But soon it was Monday, and from the nature of the preparation in progress it seemed more like an expedition. The neglected farm had facilitated the prolific reproduction of squirrels and other wild animals, so forcing the proprietor into a state of bewilderment. According to plan, Luther called at George's house around ten o'clock in the morning and we all set off, each with a shot-gun and haversack, cartridges, sandwiches, first-aid kit, a container full of drinking water and other items of necessity. To my great surprise, not a single dog was included in this venture. On enquiry, George said that he does not want to shoot a dog; one bit him once.

We stood at the entrance to the farm for a moment, then came a third man who immediately dispelled the air of apprehension which appeared to have hung over the area. Gerry, the newcomer, gaunt with beady eyes, of very dark shiny complexion, and affable, gave a quick glance up at the sky and across the farm and said, 'Right, let's go! Follow me and we'll break up a bit, when we get to the big tree.'

George and Luther willingly agreed and I followed them, not knowing what he really meant. But I was confident that George could be trusted.

'I see you have someone new with you,' Gerry remarked.

'Yes, he arrived on Saturday from Trinidad for a week's holiday,' George responded as he hacked his way through an overgrown path.

I had heard George and Luther the previous night, speak of Gerry as being the 'Guru' of the group of estates in the area, and of the particular farm on which our hunt was about to begin. He had a high-pitched nasal voice, and resolved to conserve it despite a seemingly friendly disposition. An air of mystery underlay it all.

Momentarily, we arrived at our dispersal point with instructions to reassemble at a particular rendezvous within thirty minutes. We thus pursued our respective paths with confidence, knowing that in case of doubt or difficulty, warning shots in the air must be fired, without delay.

There was ample evidence that the farm was very much neglected, and I began to wonder whether the animal life there was similar to that of the forest with which I was familiar at home. Buzzing sounds in the undergrowth were not altogether unfamiliar, but I'd never been alone before in an unknown forest. And a forest indeed it was; at that moment more like a jungle, despite its history of having been once a thriving fruit and sugar-cane plantation. It may have been in olden days.

The assault had begun. I suddenly felt apprehensive, but dared not turn back without even attempting to venture into the wilderness. Immediately, darting squirrels caught my attention. I levelled my shot gun and followed a sprightly one through the air, on to a branch of a nearby tree, down the trunk and off in the undergrowth. I had not fired at anything on the move before, not even at the pace of a hedgehog, let alone an object that moved so quickly through the air, landing on a branch and shooting along its trunk, non-stop, and away. I admired the agility of that clever little animal, and when a few moments later, in pursuing the opposite course, it paused at a forked branch to look at me, I did not even bat an eyelid and was tempted to say, 'Encore'.

After holding my original course for about fifteen minutes, I veered to the right and proceeded straight ahead as directed, to take me to the rendezvous at the appointed time. About five minutes after veering to the right, there was a noticeable absence of animal life, and no singing or fluttering of birds could be heard. A great uneasiness swept over me, and now I dared not ignore the crisp and hurried rustlings in the thick undergrowth.

Visions of the venomous viper that charges like a coiled spring, and the boa constrictor that constricts itself around the body and throat of its victim, squeezing out its last breath of life, loomed large in my imagination. Deeply buried in my mind such tales so far had risen to the surface in my thoughts, and continued unbroken for quite a while. And so I saw a vivid imagery of the largest boa constrictors, at the point of death of its victim, releasing its coil and puking up its slimy brewage of vile vomit upon it before its total engorgement.

All during that period of gruesome thoughts, instinctively, I continued my struggle against surprisingly tough undergrowth, and no sooner had I dismissed from my mind the tenor of such gruesome jungle episodes than a series of deep mournful grunts and groans began to emerge from the depth of a grimy gutter a few yards before me, partly overgrown. In my fright, I caught a glimpse of a passing object at the corner of my eye. Instantly, I raised my gun and fired. I could not possibly have been rated as a good shot by any standard, but the frightened squirrel had hesitated a fraction of a second too long, and it was no more.

How very sad I was to have lost a friend, one whom I admired not so long ago, I thought to myself. But a few minutes later, on reflection, to my great relief, the squirrel with which I exchanged glances, had a very fluffy tail and in his spritely and spirited dash, must have been more than ten miles away, I concluded.

The report from my gun had drawn three shots from my colleagues in response, and I recollected at once that it was the signal we had agreed should anyone be in danger or in any form of difficulty. Occasional whimpering human-like voice now seemed to accompany the intermittent groans; there were yet no signs of life in the region. My hair stood on end as I fired three warning shots in the air, followed by another three, and another three. I had an ample supply of cartridges, and was quite prepared to fire the charges. A strange feeling had beset me and I began threshing about the bushes in search of the direction that would lead me to the agreed meeting place. Meanwhile, shots from my colleagues were fired, almost continually as I hacked my way towards them with the rusty cutlass I carried unsheathed at my waist.

Faint hooping calls grew louder and louder, bringing cheerful tidings to my heart which, but a little while ago, had sunken to my boots with an agonising flutter.

The whole affair had a hypnotic effect upon me, and momentarily I'd completely forgotten my whereabouts. I could not remember in whose company I was, and what was the purpose for being in that location in the first place. In my dilemma, I just stood there firing my shot-gun into the air, reloading and firing, until I distinctly heard Gerry's voice saying, 'Right O! Right O! Right O! Stay where you are! Just stay where you are!'

I saw him weaving his way nimbly through the bushes towards me as though it were his natural habitat. I was very delighted indeed, but somehow the moment of my greatest triumph occurred during the firing of my shot-gun. I had repeated aloud an ancient prayer which was given to me, and I had sensed the presence of my oversoul (Lamont). The firing of the shot-gun was instinctive as breathing, I realized the futility of the exercise.

George and Luther had waited at the rendezvous where we were eventually reunited. It was only then that I realized the extent of the anxiety that had been aroused in the minds of my companions. And there was added relief, for the sun had begun its rapid descent. We returned to George Morello's home where we spent the evening, leisurely discussing the events of our enterprise.

I learned that the main reason for the neglect of the particular estate was the fact that certain regions were notoriously disreputable, and many who perchance ventured beyond bounds had been driven to insanity. Worse still, others had met their death mysteriously. The estate was haunted.

George apologised for allowing me to set off without being accompanied. According to his direction, I ought to have been the first to arrive at the rendezvous. Gerry, the 'Guru', after waiting for a while there, assumed that I must have veered to the opposite direction and decided to go in search of me, leaving George and Luther at the meeting place in case I turned up. As it was, Gerry had saved the day, and perhaps my life.

Silently thinking the matter over to myself, I began to believe that there must be some validity in many of the weird ancient ghouls who prance and dance about among themselves in the dark of the night killing the intruder with dire fright. I therefore declined all further hunting expeditions from that day.

On my return back to work in the drawing-office, I made a re-appraisal of my position, and my long-time ambition to study medicine sprung to life. It was my desire, in any case, to pursue a university education. I forthwith informed close members of my family.

During the period of my friendship with the twin-sisters, I continued as usual with my regular duties, both at home and at work in the normal way, and kept up a lively interest in the social activities of our village, including the improvement of the band. With the inclusion of new members, we had moved away from purely calypso music to include various types of jazz and Latin American music. I continued to retain the leadership.

As the Oil Company continued its expansion, more and more people moved into the district and the demands of the Village Band had increased accordingly. Excursions by bus and by train to the various seaside resorts with the band in attendance were commonplace. And there were the customary weddings, christenings and parties at various homes for one type of celebration or another – birthdays, anniversaries – requesting the services of the band.

I was the leader from its inception and having grown up in a community where everybody was related to nearly everybody, it was very difficult to refuse a polite and friendly request, and it was all free of charge. We played music solely for the pleasure and that which it gave to others. Most requests were initiated by the women folk, and directed to me. This may have accounted for my so-called popularity.

During this period too I became acquainted with one of

the newcomers to our district, and being very interested in music, she took a lively interest in the band, and in my clarinet playing in particular. I was nearly twenty-nine. She frequently visited our home and was liked by all the members of our family, my father in particular. She knew of my plans and my dedication to further my studies, and gave encouragement towards the achievement of my goal. In due course we got married. I eventually left for the United Kingdom to further my education.

At a very early stage of my childhood when black and white people congregated at religious ceremonies in the church, it was obvious to the whole community that the whites had both right of way and right of place in all matters. And this was particularly noticeable in the organising of bazaars and such fund-raising issues. They were, of course, the better educated, better off economically, and seemingly, in every other respect. That was an accepted fact about which no grudge was borne, but their overbearing superior air and oppressive attitude as a whole towards black people ensured that the status quo was rigidly maintained.

In the circumstances, all black people were made to feel inferior and I assumed that the apparent superiority was due solely to their education and wealth, of course. On that assumption, I was determined to educate myself in whatever way possible, and eventually to pursue a university education.

I believed then that poor people as a whole were looked down upon because they lacked the necessary education for their advancement. My resolve was therefore strengthened.

242

34

Old Village Exodus

I look back upon the old village of Pointe-à-Pierre as I knew it in the days of my childhood, and see myself and other children growing up among caring, pleasant and generous community which comprised our village folk. Many adults, on recounting, like myself, would consider their lives in those days as being full of the glory that had been derived from so many adventurous and exciting pursuits in a multi-racial community enriched by their respective traditions and cultures.

The elders of the village in those days were regarded with great respect, and by their general demeanour set a seal of conduct over the whole village. And with every adult having the right to discipline any child anywhere as necessary, it could be said that in a way, a quasi vigilance had been the order of the day. It must be said that the community as a whole, was remarkably industrious and resilient.

These features were clearly exemplified by the need to divert attention to the oil industry from agriculture and fishing, and the greatest test of all was exacted at the time of great expansion by the Company which precipitated our 'compulsory' evacuation from the old village.

The mass exodus from the old homes brought about a swift and sudden end to the old order of life. But, with several of the former inhabitants, including myself, long

243

engaged with the firm, new accommodation was acquired in close surroundings.

In time, a considerable number of employees from the former village of Pointe-à-Pierre had progressed with the firm and had proved themselves capable of holding positions of high office, long before the colonial regime had been dismantled, in 1962, the year of Independence.

It was believed that the oil refinery at Pointe-à-Pierre was opened in 1914. (See appropriate history books for details). I was only three years of age, and grew to be of service to the firm for the first nineteen and a half years of my working life. It was a service which was officially regarded as highly commendable from the firm's point of view. Such acclaim most certainly would not have been expressed had I given vent to my feelings in respect of the numerous injustices I had endured over those long and impressionable years of my life. Nevertheless, I learned much. For that I was thankful. Tolerance and self-discipline were among my greatest achievements.

The industry seemed always to be expanding, and most certainly undergoing maintenance and renovation of some sort. In 1938, the firm had embarked on massive development projects and as such was better prepared to cope with the boom years of the industry during World War II. As a result, several generations arising from or related to former inhabitants of the old village played their part in the production and refinement of one of the world's most precious commodities of modern times, and will have been privileged to occupy some of the high offices unthinkable in bygone days.

The local white community, some of whom were born on the island, had lived in the new exclusive part of the district. This community constituted the upper-class and controlled the economic structure of the entire district. It was not until some time after I had begun working at the machine-shop that I became aware of their presence, and their overriding influence.

Although every white person was a member of the upper-class, those who were natives of the island were at an inferior level in their society to the native European at that time; and the blacks or non-whites were at the bottom of the scale in general rating, irrespective of their educational attainments.

This is a simplification of the social structure. As far as I knew, whites and non-whites had no overt social contact at that time. Hence, with a great number of staff (whites) and employees (non whites) engaged in an expanding oil industry, the interplay of the numerous unseen forces may well be gauged.

The Company always seemed to have been in the process of expansion, acquiring new lands and new sites for various projects. One such occasion had involved all the members working at the drawing-office. An entire new building had been provided on a new site overlooking a golf course about one mile away from the old site. In this new environment, I had seen a man walking towards a green quite leisurely, and was suddenly struck down, or rather, burnt down, in bright daylight. He was engulfed in bluish-green smoke which was preceded by a blinding streak of lightning. I had witnessed the occurrence only weeks after moving into the new office. It was a staggering phenomenon, and for a moment I wondered whether he had recently committed some ghastly offence.

Fairly frequently, it seemed to me at the time, there were terrifying explosions followed by screaming fire engines and an ambulance, sometimes two or more in quick succession.

This new office was virtually at the periphery of the oil refineries with their high-pressure furnaces, chemical laboratories and several major plants, constantly humming their characteristic melancholic melodies. It was in such environment that I spent most of my nineteen and a half years in the employ of the most productive oil refining company in the island – the district of my birth.

But the areas of greatest hazards at that time were in the vicinities of the high pressure furnaces, situated in the heart of the 'Cracking Plants'. The crude oil was pumped to the respective plant in the 'raw state' from oil-wells several miles away, and heated to a very high temperature by passing it through the furnace under pressure in coils of steel tubing. At the appropriate temperature, the product was pumped up into a tall steel chamber at the uppermost section. The steel chamber was referred to as the Fractionating Tower (or column). As the name implied, the various fractions in the tower roughly separate and settle according to their respective densities, the lightest being at the top and the heaviest at the bottom. In those days, of course, the fraction most suitable for aviation spirit would be located at the top section of the tower. The various fractions were drawn off at the predetermined levels and pumped to the respective plants for purification and refinement. From this simple explanation, the possible consequences of the amount of inflammable products in a highly-charged atmosphere could well be imagined.

Shortly after moving into the new office, I was made a full draughtsman and a tracer was assigned to me, for an additional amount of field work had been in my charge. The newly established practice of transferring apprentices to the drawing-office for training in the art of reading mechanical drawings, had just been extended to white apprentice engineers. In addition, arrangements were made for them to develop their skills in a variety of field work.

One morning a young man joined the Drawing Office

staff. He was eighteen, the latest apprentice engineer recruit, and was assigned to me in order to acquaint himself with the various types of field work – involving the use of the theodolite and level in land-surveying. He was a white youth, and a native of the island as were his parents. He had accompanied me on several occasions, and willingly held the staff for me, but only in out-of-the-way places where he was not likely to be seen by anyone, particularly a white person.

There was an occasion, however, when a crucial elevation had to be established from a particular bench-mark for the installation of an important compressor. There were the fitters at the foundation site waiting for the information from me. He became red in the face and refused to hold the staff for me. He made several lame excuses and finally pretended to be ill and walked away. We were not in the open country. Here, we had an audience of fitters waiting in readiness to make fast their foundation bolts. That was too daunting a prospect for the apprentice engineer because more eyes than usual were focused upon him. And there were also white onlookers.

I continued my correspondence course, frequently studying up to the small hours of the morning, but I found it necessary to shift the emphasis to the study of reinforced concrete construction. I therefore purchased the necessary books on the projects that were under way. They comprised retaining walls, roofs, bridges and culverts. This diversion necessitated a break from my course which was further prolonged by the depth of involvement in this new project.

Offshore survey of the seabed had to be carried out in order to facilitate the accommodation of large oil tankers, and thus cope with the increased demand for the export of oil. The survey of the seabed was necessary to determine the extent of dredging that had to be undertaken, not only to ensure that the water in the particular area would be deep enough but because a pipeline viaduct of considerable length had to be constructed to convey the refined products from the refineries and the various plants to the tankers at the island jetty.

The word 'oil' was used in general terms. The word 'fuel' would have been more appropriate, for the products comprised aviation spirit, gasoline, kerosene, paraffin, lubricating oil, and a host of by-products.

The whole project was executed with a great deal of interest and excitement, and participation in such work thereafter became part of my routine engagement.

The affairs of my immediate family continued to prosper. My father had retired from his back-breaking occupation as a plate-layer with the Government Railways, and had taken the much more leisurely task of occasional fishing and gardening as it suited him.

Music was an essential element in the lives of the people of our village and of the country as a whole. The band had increased in numbers and had attained a reputable standard of proficiency, and its versatility had been a great bonus.

Meanwhile, of course, the expansion of the oil refinery continued in full flourish, and the Company's quest for additional lands had taken them eastwards, then southwards, and towards the west. And now, set for what may have been their greatest enterprise in the acquisition of land, a big push northwards had been executed. This venture inflicted untold misery upon the people of our village, of a kind hitherto unexperienced, and not everyone had been able to survive the ordeal with its insidious implication. Our old village had ultimately vanished in the big push to the north of their establishment.

The main north-south road ran virtually parallel to the coast line about 400 yards away. There were houses on

248

both sides of the road for a distance of about 880 yards. The residents on the west side of the main road (nearer the sea) had a commanding view of the coastline and immediate access to the sea. In that very region nestled the beautiful Campeche Bay which the fishermen of the village, including my father, and generations before them, had used in the pursuit of their livelihood. It was there, too, that I had learned to swim. The entrance to the path which led to the sea was situated opposite our house, and I recall the pleasure I derived from looking up from our front garden at two tall palm trees nearby, and admiring birds in playful mood, singing their hearts out in nonchalant flirtation. The palm trees, tall and elegant, were like sentinels of an ancient civilization entrusted with the safeguard of the community's legacy to posterity – an abiding peace and prosperity. But, alas, it was not to be!

In one fell swoop, all the residences on the west side of the main road were served with notices to vacate the land. The Oil Company had acquired it and they were the landlords. Despite objections and protests, the plans of the Company were rigidly executed. The tenants were at the mercy of landlords who, over the years, had long been their employers at one plant or another; most of the tenants held important positions in laboratories and offices. Thus vexatious frowning at the notices to vacate the land was not advised for those who wished to retain their jobs and prosper with the firm. As it turned out, the whole of that area overlooking the sea was earmarked for residential quarters to house the company's elite staff. Now with the vast majority of the tenants already in secure jobs with the firm, it was easy to imagine what would have been the outcome if anyone had dared to raise a stubborn resistance.

But not everyone was employed with the Company, and such persons were less inclined to heed the notice to vacate the land, despite the legal implication. Most of the elderly belonged to this category. They were mostly of the older generation who no longer had a family, and yet were a predominant factor in the elusive matter of heritage and posterity. Nevertheless, their chances against so powerful a firm were utterly ineffectual, and after removal of the last house, hut or shack, the bulldozers, in due course, thundered over that land, raising veils of dust in their rampage. There were many people whose houses were too fragile for refabrication. They suffered tremendous misery and heartache, for many were in tears and brooding long before the expiratory date of their notices.

Within an incredibly short space of time, luxurious bungalows set well back from the main road sprawled over the area, gaily flaunting their excellence. There were a vast number of places on the west side of the road that were favourite hiding places from which, as children, we shot out and ran into the sea. I had long passed that playful stage, but lack of free access to the sea had concerned me and, most of all, the many encumbrances. Stark display of notices with threat of prosecution for trespassers seemed strangely sinister and utterly abhorrent. But, it was a lawful undertaking.

Those of us who lived on the east side of the main road had considered ourselves most fortunate, for we were assured that we would not be affected by the change they were about to make.

I was living on the east side with my father and brothers at the famous corner subsequently named after my father, and figured so prominently in my scooter accident. Having had a first hand account of the misery and degradation of the West Side exodus, I appreciated all the more our good fortune of being left unperturbed. But, after a relatively short period, it was rumoured that the Company was planning to serve us with notice to vacate the whole of the area East of the North-South main road, in another surge of their expansion programme.

One morning during this period of uncertainty, Hana, whose role in the village was reputed to be that of a kindly busy-body, was certainly in her element. She was not unlike a self-appointed 'lookout bird' in a bird sanctuary. A wiry middle-aged woman, long widowed and incapable of readjustment, she busied herself by picking up snippets of news here and there and putting them together at random. This habit had frequently generated shock and consternation in the village. But despite it all, she was considered to be a good and friendly old soul . . . well-meaning in many ways.

Having spotted some furtive manoeuvrings in the distance that morning, Hana, lowering her diminutive figure, rushed through her back garden and along a footpath, negotiating a sharp bend up an incline with surprising agility for a woman of her age. Hastily knocking on Paul's front door which he always left ajar, she called out excitedly, 'Paul, Paul, I'm coming in, cover up yourself!'

'Hey, hey, Hana, what's all this about now?' Paul asked, but Hana had already entered his house. 'Who's following you!' he asked sharply.

'Nobody, nobody,' Hana replied briskly, in a lowered tone of voice. 'Come, look over there . . . no, no! Not there, over there, look!' she asserted, easing the window open a trifle wider.

Paul reminded her that he didn't like his window wide open, and that he was able to see all he wanted through the cracks in the walls. They were both of mixed blood – Negro and Indian – with black hair loosely curled.

'Ah didn't come to pick a quarrel, you know, Paul.'

'Well, what then?'

Hana directed him to the largest opening near the

window and told him to take a good look, then tell her what he saw. Paul looked in silence, shifting his head slightly to get a better view. When he was satisfied, he agreed with Hana that the men he had just seen approaching were the same two men who had brought the notices around to the tenants on the other side of the main road. The men had moved swiftly, for within seconds there was a double pounding on the front door of Paul's house. Hana shuddered and retreated into a corner of the room.

Paul answered the knock at the door and received a hand-to-hand notice to vacate the land. Hana was right; it was bad news for everyone East of the Main Road. After a moment of quivering silence, Paul consoled Hana and told her that she was still young, but he, at eighty-two, had nowhere to go. He further explained that he was an old fool for believing that they would be left alone. He saw no sense in living, and would rather die. There was another period of silence, then suddenly Paul hurried over to the window and craned his neck. He had flung the window wide open and had seen the two men still on their mission, handing out the notices.

Repeating the statement that he would rather die, he shouted: 'Shoot me now, shoot me now!' as he pushed open the door bared his chest and set off in pursuit of the two messengers, demanding to be shot on the spot.

After a great commotion, the residents settled down and arranged their affairs, using the experience of those who left before, to their advantage.

Imagine: the day the razing of the land was scheduled to begin. The golden rays of the morning sun played upon the menacing bulldozers patiently awaiting the crucial moment. From their rendezvous on the crest of a ridge, their long shadows, shortening with the rising sun, appeared like evil monsters as a stark reminder of their destructive capability. The complete destruction of the village was now imminent, and the gruesome drama of a short while ago was about to be repeated. The consequences were far greater. All the pleadings and wailings typical of human tragedy and sufferings were swept aside. That's how it seemed ... the emotional scars are inexplicable.

In due course, there was not a vestige of the life I knew except for an odd mango or orange tree, and very few landmarks left to tell the tale. It was a deep and sorrowful reality. The peaceful and beautiful fishing village as I knew it had completely disappeared.

Sometimes I used to reflect upon the ancient tales I had heard as a child, and was carried away, wondering if angels did really congregate on the Mont and sang soft, sweet melodies in the cool of the night. It was reasonable to believe that no such stories would ever be told again in the village for with its 'life' abandoned, would have vanished with the wind and the dust, all traces of posterity.

In adapting to the new situation, several families, including my own, moved to a new estate in the district of Marabella, South of the Company's establishment. It was a very expedient move (a vivid realisation on one of my father's remarks in times of disappointment – 'What happens, happens for the better') for I was now situated closer to my place of work, and the chances of having to move house again were rather remote.

The rapid influx of tenants into this new estate, however, soon created an agonising problem. The landlords of the new estate, seeking to maximise their profits, had increased the rent of their property to an alarming degree. In order to safeguard our interests, a Tenants' Association was organised. This necessitated the promotion of open-air meetings at street corners and other public places in order to arouse the interest of the community.

I was elected President of the Association and with a very diligent and capable secretary the Association had grown to exert a marked restraining influence upon the landlord.

Apart from our close co-operation in the affairs of the Association, a few colleagues and I worked arduously on our respective preparation for the London Matriculation Examination in order to further our education abroad.

35

Frustrations

At length, I received a long-awaited rise in pay. It was disappointingly small, with promise of a further rise within the next few months. The tragic effect of the disappointment generated new ideas into my mind. At the drawing-office an Asian gentleman occupied a drawing-table adjacent to mine. He was a highly qualified engineer with several post-graduate qualifications to his credit. He had attained University degrees from London, Canada and the United States of America, and yet his salary as Consultant Engineer was less than that of European draughtsmen. The fact that such a highly qualified person was kept at such a low salary was, for me, a very daunting prospect and I was only a draughtsman, first-class though I may have been.

Furthermore, on Sports' Day Celebrations organised by the Company, the only black persons who were privileged to occupy a place on the grand stand were those of the medical, dental and legal professions. On the whole members of those professions were usually self-employed and their salaries did not depend upon stringent regulations which, in many cases, arose from colour prejudice, favouritism or some other preferential considerations.

At that stage, time appeared to move very slowly, and after a great deal of thought I finally decided to study medicine, or at any rate one of the professions. A whole year has passed and I was twenty-nine. In the circumstances, I immediately applied for admission to Universities in the United Kingdom to pursue a course in medicine. From their replies I learned, with great disappointment and surprise, that I had to obtain a certificate for having passed the London Matriculation Examination or the equivalent. Fortunately, I had begun reading my chosen subjects, not really knowing that a certificate was essential for admission to a University.

In the circumstances I decided to seek proper tuition and got down to serious work. I sent away to England for a correspondence course in my five chosen subjects: English, mathematics, dynamics, geometrical and mechanical drawing and Spanish. I had grown accustomed to studying by correspondence and I looked forward to the course with great excitement.

Meanwhile, I was appointed Instructor on the subject of geometrical drawing at an Institute in the principal town of the south. Knowing that my acceptance would contribute to my success at the London Matriculation Examination, I applied myself accordingly. But gradually I became disenchanted with my work as a draughtsman for the firm. This feeling was totally at variance with my character, for I had always discharged my duty with enthusiasm. I therefore decided to seek a similar position with another oil company. I was successful in obtaining a job, about twenty miles away, and so I handed in my resignation, after eighteen years of continuous service.

I had taken some examples of my work on the occasion of my interview for the new job, and was offered nearly twice the salary I was being paid. Two or three days after handing in my resignation, the Chief Draughtsman requested me to call him at his office to discuss the matter of my leaving for a new job. At the interview I was told to cancel my application to the other oil company with the promise of an immediate rise in salary, and that they would get in touch with the new firm to smooth over matters.

It was not until one month had passed that I received the rise that had been promised, but it was a mere ten per cent instead of nearly double my salary as had been agreed by the new firm. The position with the new firm had been completely closed against me. I received a letter from them telling me that they could not deprive a sister company of one of their best men. The actors in the 'Play' must have busied themselves because the new firm had not yet received my letter of cancellation before my old firm wrote to me. I was a closed chapter.

The 'Corridor Incident' was demoralising, and somehow I couldn't help superimposing this incident upon it. In many ways, it was far worse.

I began work as a 'boy' at fifteen and a half with the firm, and to the powers that were, at thirty-two I was still a boy. In such a situation, the possibility of obtaining a similar position with another firm anywhere on the Island was absolutely nil.

On the occasion of the 'Corridor Incident', I was a boy. But at thirty-two I had weathered countless number of storms of high-force winds, blowing hot and cold at times, from numerous directions, often at the same time. After all that, to be debarred from what I considered an opportunity of a lifetime was devastating, to say the least. There was nothing I could have done but suffer in silence.

I reflected upon several instances when a member of white draughtsman faced with difficult mathematical problems relating to some structural design, condescended to seek my assistance. On the approach of a senior official, the over-friendly gesture vanished as suddenly as the mountain mist that had been chased by the glowing warmth of an unbridled tropical sun. There were always technical problems to be solved and I enjoyed tackling them as well as helping others in doing so.

World War II was more than half way through by this time, and I prayed that it would be over soon. My resolve to work steadfastly at my subjects had been strengthened in that way. In due course I sat the examination and failed. Without loss of heart, I sat it later and passed in only three of the five subjects. I continued further preparation without a pause, by correspondence from a college in Oxford, England.

I continued to maintain high interest in my work and had paid great attention to economic living, for all my personal savings had to be directed to my education abroad. Many of my friends and relatives were in possession of their own motor cars and other luxury goods, but I decided to pursue higher education and was prepared to pay for it. I had no alternative.

News of the end of the War in 1945 was greeted with great rejoicing. I was particularly delighted, and not only for humanity's sake, but for the earliest opportunity to obtain admission to a university in Britain. But the dismantling of the elaborate paraphernalia of the world conflict had cheated me of precious time and it was not until August 1946 that I was able to obtain a passage to England. As soon as I had purchased my travel ticket and received information of the ship's arrival at Port of Spain Harbour, I handed in my resignation, with much greater confidence than on the previous occasion.

Again I was requested to see the Chief Draughtsman in his office. I sat facing him at his desk as he looked at my letter of resignation lying before him.

'I see you're leaving,' he said, 'have you got another job?' he added quickly.

I explained that I was not going to another job, but that

I was going to the United Kingdom to further my education. Surprise and disbelief shone over his countenance, and I produced my ticket to Southampton to bring quickly to an end the attempted repetition of a disconsolate air.

He had sensed the depth of my frustration, and my resolve. References and financial settlement were hurriedly arranged, and with best wishes I took my leave in peace and harmony.

Forthwith, I strolled over to the machine-shop to inform Mr Barber in whose charge I was at the machine-shop. He received the news with mixed feelings. I informed others too. Their reaction was similar. What made them less cheerful about my decision was the fact that I did not intend to pursue engineering, as one might have imagined.

I thanked all concerned for their kindness to me when I was in the machine-shop years ago. They all wished me the best of luck.

In a further private discussion with Mr Barber a few minutes later, he expressed grave concern, not only about my going abroad, but my chosen subject. I told him that I'd given the matter careful consideration and concluded that there was no future prospect for me with the Company in the field of engineering.

'But you have a good job, and what's more you've a very good reputation, Oh, wait a minute! Are you thinking of taking up something else?' Mr Barber asked, quite puzzled.

'Yes, I'm going to study medicine if I could get into a university.'

'But why? You're a first-class engineer already. . . .'

'Oh, no, no,' I interrupted, 'and in any case, as a qualified engineer with a university degree, I would have to come back to the same employers and would be treated in just the same way as the coloured engineer who has several postgraduate university qualifications to his name. He earns only slightly more than a draughtsman from Europe, Canada or South Africa. So, you see! What prospects are there for me?' I asked.

Mr Barber nodded slowly as I spoke, giving the expression that a whole field of knowledge had just been opened up to him. He was deep in thought.

'Well,' he said after a few moments, 'I see exactly what you mean. Whatever you do, you'll succeed, I'm sure. Take care, and God bless you,' Mr Barber concluded.

Somehow, he had reinforced my justification for resigning from the firm, and had strengthened my resolve enormously.

Alex, with whom I was associated in the early days of childhood, was employed in the machine-shop where I was first engaged by the Company. He saw me speaking to the deputy foreman in whose charge I was when I started on the lathe in the machine shop. We hardly saw each other in those latter years.

Walking briskly towards me, he said, 'Hello Jacob, I hear you're leaving the job, man! So what's all that about? You're throwing away a good job like that man?' he remarked passionately with a critical air.

'How do you mean throwing my job away?' I asked.

'Well, you don't want to keep it, do you? do you? . . . am I right?'

I paused for a while, then agreed. 'Yes, you're quite right . . . quite right, Alex.'

I agreed for I was in no mood for any unnecessary argument. Alex had developed a peculiar trait of arguing over nothing of consequence. Instinctively I distanced myself from quarrelsome people, and so we drifted apart.

But, not satisfied with the simplicity of my concluding remark, Alex decided to pursue the matter.

'So, tell me this, Jacob; if you have something and you don't want it anymore, it's just like giving it away, isn't?' he asked.

Again I paused, then said, 'Well, Alex, looking at it from that point of view, I suppose you could say so . . . yes,' I agreed, nodding my head unwittingly in confirmation.

His eyes lit up and a broad smile encompassed his whole face as an expression of victory.

'Well, what are you going to do now, then?' he asked as he straightened himself to his full average adult height.

'Oh, I'm going to England.'

'What! . . . what you say?' he asserted, refusing to believe his ears.

'I'm going to England,' I repeated the sentence slowly.

'Hell! . . . that's worse,' he said with a most definitive expression. After a few moment's recovery, he asked, 'What on earth for?'

'To further my education,' I replied also in a definitive manner.

He saw no point in discussing the matter any further. We thus broke off the conversation. He wished me luck. We patted each other on the shoulder and said goodbye on good terms. Alex's view was identical with that of several other friends and colleagues on that point.

36

Reflections

Looking back upon the village of Pointe-à-Pierre and its peoples with whom I have been so closely associated, particularly in the old section of the village, in the days of my childhood, I see a quiet and contented people, mostly of African decent earning their livelihood mainly by fishing and agriculture. I see a great number of East Indians, too, and to a lesser degree, Portuguese, Spaniards and Chinese descendants. In fact, I see a number of different cultures living harmoniously in varying degrees of integration. Having said that, I should mention that the East Indians were more inclined to keep to themselves, and that was mainly on religious grounds.

I see, too, a few white people living in the highly developed southern section of the district, mainly British from the United Kingdom, and a great number of local birth. The white people represented the elite class in those days and lived exclusively in an area reserved for them. They played a prominent part in the affairs of the church so far as financial support applied, and their seats in selected pews, presumably paid for, were reserved, many of which were vacant while many of the weak and elderly at worship stood throughout, unable to obtain a seat.

All these things I see clearly through the eyes of a thirteen-year-old. And as I grew older, still in panoramic view, I see at first the gradual changes in the established practices in our midst due to the emergence of oil-refining plants, actually in the district of Pointe-à-Pierre. With the rapid development of the Oil Company, came a transformation of the village, so quickly and so involved that one hardly believed there existed the sleepy village I knew as a child. As the oil industry continued to flourish, it provided more and more employment not only for the local inhabitants, but for several people in the surrounding districts. And indeed it attracted employees from all over the country including the capital city of Port of Spain.

Marked expansion entailed the acquisition of new lands, the preparation of various sites and the installation of a vast complex of refining plants for such products as aviation spirit, different grades of gasoline, kerosene, lubrication oil and a host of by-products. And for all those products I see bulldozers at work everywhere on newly acquired land, gouging deep into the earth for the construction of large-capacity storage tanks, for the highly inflammable materials. Generally, each of these tanks made of sheets of steel, riveted or welded at the seams, was like a tomb with its own graveyard surrounded by a wall of earth in most cases, in the form of a dam.

This wall was generally referred to as the firebank, the enclosure being ten or twenty per cent greater than the capacity of the actual tank so as to ensure that the contents would be contained in the firebank, in case of fire or leakage.

Giant cranes appear here and there lunging, jerking, faltering then suddenly burying their steel fangs into a stone quarry, then gouging out a belly-full, then swinging away in a hurry and emptying their contents into waiting wagons, ready to scuttle away on miniature railways to their destination.

The construction of huge reinforced concrete piles for the support of an 'island jetty' at a depth capable of accommodating large oil tankers proved to be invaluable during the war period, when all efforts were mobilised to maximise output in every department of the industry. In the preparation to extend the existing 'island jetty', giant dredgers dug deep into the seabed, clearing the entrance at the approaches for the world's largest tankers at that time. And the speedy construction of a major pipeline viaduct extending from the shore to the new extension jetty ensured the maximum supply of fuel to numerous tankers on call.

At the height of activity, barges and tugs, small ships and large ships seemed to mingle and criss-cross with motor launches and speed boats in some sort of organised disorder. Every aspect of that enterprise bristled with activity, both at sea and on land, by day and by night in a relentless hustle and bustle. And when the tubes of a furnace became choked, minimum time was spent in making it fit for use again by suitable steel reamers operated under the pressure of compressed air.

I still hear the sound of a thousand roaring bulls, and see engineers with safety helmets and goggles, and cumbersome gloves and overalls, gently coaxing their air-driven reamers back and forth through each of the multitude of tubes in their charge, night and day as necessary.

There were accidents, minor, major and fatal, too. A tube head from a furnace is blown off at high-pressure, clearing anything in its path with a resulting inferno instantly reddening the sky, which, at night, could be seen very many miles around, just as, indeed, on a quiet night, the explosion would be heard. The plant's siren immediately sets off the alarm, and this is joined by the Company's ambulances and fire engines with powerful sirens of their own, adding considerable tension to the mounting anxiety. Relatives and friends of the employees engaged on the plant in question suffer the agony of suspense, pending an official declaration as to the outcome of the misadventure.

I see the Company's expansion programme take another leap forward, and the land on which the houses of the poorer inhabitants of the northern section of the village, pass with great anguish, into the 'hands' of the Oil Company. Naturally, being in the thick of it all, I see and feel the effects anew. But time continued its onward march and I see myself resettled with members of our family and others from Pointe-à-Pierre, on a new estate in Marabella, much closer to my place of work. By many, it must have been said to be a blessing in disguise.

Several months later when the dust from the exodus was settled, there was an incidental meeting of heads from some of the old folk whose removal from Pointe-à-Pierre had also been enforced. In the exchange of ideas that ensued, an elder, who was generally regarded as a 'quiet thinker', was praised by many of his colleagues and contemporaries for his optimism during the period of deprivation occasioned by the notices served upon the inhabitants in question.

The 'quiet thinker' in question had always taken the view that: 'Everything is good, and what happens, happens for the better'. My father was looked upon as 'the quiet thinker', and that must have been his way of dealing with unavoidable circumstances.

Despite the many inconveniences, humiliation, and degradation at times, at the hands of a few members of the all-white staff of the Oil Company, there was no doubt that industrialisation of the area had brought enormous benefits to us all. And not only to the local inhabitants, but to the island in general.

In my particular case, by listening, observing and discreetly copying the general behaviours of the more refined Europeans, especially the Chief Draughtsman – an English gentleman – I learned a great deal in respect of my personal demeanour and manner of speech.

Above all, the innovation of the oil industry in the area provided employment for a vast number of people from all walks of life. And for many, the opportunity of learning a trade or some other form of occupation was of paramount importance. In the process, the heightening of one's ambition was inevitable, and, like myself, there were employees who, despite great difficulties, had worked persistently and arduously towards their betterment. Eventually, they gained admission to universities in the United States of America, the United Kingdom, and in other European countries.

I was thirty-five, and had reached the stage of total disenchantment with my position as Assistant Engineer, Drawing and Design, with the Company. I therefore took a bold step to improve my position. The only way out was to go to England, in my view; and so arrangements for my passage were put in hand. I then awaited transport by ship.

As the hour of my departure drew closer, I couldn't help wondering what impression the average observer would have of the village of Pointe-à-Pierre, taking into account its peoples, or rather their dispersal from the old section, and the expansive growth of the oil industry into a gigantic complex involving thousands of people in the task for their livelihood. An aerial view in daylight at the height of activity would now have revealed scores of chimney stacks towering into the sky, emitting smoke of contrasting colours, drifting towards the sea by the prevailing wind. And to those pollutants would be added, in abundance, the toxic fumes and vapours consistent

266

with the production of innumerable by-products manu-factured in specialised plants dispersed over wide areas.

Inflammable gases that were incapable of being harnessed were piped 'out of bounds' and burnt off. With plants in full operation, each day and night of the week, unwittingly, one would be inclined to associate the issuing of the flame with the Olympic Torch, and the torch resident at the Arc de Triomphe in Paris, despite the gross disparity in the nobleness of their cause.

The patient observer would add to his list dazzling reflections from reservoirs of various shapes and sizes. These ensure adequate supply of water, not only for domestic use, but for industrial purpose, including the needs of the Company's elaborate fire-fighting apparatus. Streaming vapour from huge cooling towers catch the eye from afar, and a close inspection of a plant occasionally reveals a counterpart in miniature, escaping from a defective joint, hissing under pressure. Each plant spoke a language peculiar to itself, and its operator was the Master Interpreter.

In the eyes of a young adult, I saw Pointe-à-Pierre as a fascinating village in the early days before the massive shift of labour from the land to the oil industry. I saw a tough, industrious, enterprising, resilient and endearing community, throwing in their lot, one with another to help the other; the whole rendering assistance where necessary. The entire exercise constituted a commend-able example of gallantry.

Access to the sea facilitated the export of essential refined products to countries all over the world. Re-dredged water lanes were provided to accommodate many of the world's cargo ships alongside what were termed 'island jetties'. These jetties, as the term implies, were constructed as far out into the sea as possible. They were in effect terminals as platforms at the end of a complex pipeline viaduct. Thus ships supplied and discharged their cargo.

Such enormous undertakings by the Oil Company, with its extensive housing projects, ensured steady employment for all members of the community, black and white; all working towards a common goal – the maximum production of one of the world's most precious commodities. Towards that end, despite its status as a small island, Trinidad had already established itself among the oil producers of the world.

At the period under review, the unbiased observer, speculating, would conclude that in the light of circumstances, the line of demarcation between the two sections of Point-à-Pierre and its peoples would, one day, be completely eroded and a fully integrated community would emerge, and would be sure to add, 'The sooner the better.'

Many a wild rose is wilfully destroyed by man – the world loses beauty and bees and humming birds die from lack of nectar. Frequently I saw my colleagues beaten and humiliated by their supervisors and considered 'dead and done with' as far as their prospects of job-promotion were concerned. The motive was prejudice of one form or another.

At the age of thirty-four, completely disillusioned, in 1946 I finally decided to try for a university education which would take me away from the humiliations at the oil refinery. Most of all, I was determined that I would not be crushed or dedicated. I saw further education as a necessary step, so I resigned and booked a passage to England.

In August 1946 I travelled the thirty-four miles by train to Port of Spain, the Island's capital. I had made the journey several times before, but on this occasion I thought of the train rushing over the hundreds of sleepers my father had helped to lay during his plate-laying days with the Railway Authority. I was not a stranger to the harbour for I had often seen large oil-tankers and other cargo ships at berth, loading and off-loading; but I was essentially a country man. Always I was bemused by the city life with all its hustle and bustle. The capital was totally different from the village and there were people, and more people, and yet more people everywhere. I caught a glimpse of a striking figure disappearing into the crowd. I was moving towards the ticket office and the man at the same time. Suddenly my cousin Lewis and I came face to face. He was a venerable elder of our village.

'Hello Jacob!' he greeted me with a broad smile and an affectionate embrace.

'Oh, cousin Lewis, I'm so pleased to see you; I intended to get in touch. . . .'

'Never mind, my boy, you're so busy . . . I always enquire about you. I've heard the good news, and indeed I hoped to see you during my few days in the capital – just to say hello and give you my blessing,' my cousin remarked with joy and admiration.

I felt myself fortunate for in those days such deeds were performed with great reverence.

'Thank you, cousin Lewis; I know you always have my interest at heart and I'm truly grateful. You said you had heard the good news . . . Why did you say it's good news?'

'Well, for what it's worth, furthering your education is the best thing to do.'

'What do you mean by "for what it's worth"?'

Cousin Lewis was a down-to-earth man who had no truck with sentimentality or hypotheses.

He looked at me fixedly with his dark-brown sparkling eyes and said, 'Well, suppose you study engineering and come back here, you'll have the same bosses, and you'll get the same sort of treatment even though you'd be better

269

qualified than most ... you see what I mean?' he remarked with great emphasis.

I was totally in agreement and even more delighted that I had not intended to study engineering. He gave me his blessing and we separated into the crowd.

Flooding over the harbour and its approaches were people, pushing and straining against each other and the port officials. Despite the crush there was little ill-temper apart from the occasional dramatic outburst when someone was accidentally pushed off balance and perchance a toe with an aching corn was trodden on. But even so, such explosions of temper were brief.

The great attraction at the harbour was the presence of a sleek troop-ship berthed at the pier in readiness to take the passengers across the Caribbean Sea and into the Gulf of Mexico. It was thought that the ship had been commissioned to take demobilised service men back to their respective countries. I was ushered through the ship's corridors with an air of great secrecy. I could not see the reason for this and everyone seemed too nervous to speak in more than a whisper. I had the strange feeling that the ship may have been fitted with some extra-sensory device which could automatically register one's deepest thoughts. It was eerie.

When the signal for boarding had been announced, I had wasted no time in securing a vantage point on deck. I was early and so had ample time to relax and to reflect and let my mind wander as it pleased. But, the swelling crowd on the quayside arrested my attention as the streamlined warship arresting theirs.

Amongst them, were women flaunting, awkwardly, the coquetry of youth they had long outlived. But then there were others, whose long silken hair floated freely in the breeze, rippling as obstinately as the brooklet from a mountain spring. Then too, there were men, women and

270

children gazing opened-mouthed at the ship which they imagined had taken their relatives and friends to the battle field and did not bring them back . . .

Now, deep in the bowels of the ship, vibrant life began to stir. The hour of our departure was imminent, and it seemed as though a vast new generation had joined the admiring throng. There was great jubilation heightened by an occasional blast from the ship which always drew the crowd closer together, waving incessantly. For the poet or painter, novelist or playwright and indeed, for all who admired human faces for what they told of human experiences, a golden opportunity was right there at hand. Looking superior were those whose sons and daughter had won coveted Island Scholarships which entitled them to take degree courses at virtually any university of their choice, and these at nominal cost. A blast from the ship's siren unsettled the crowd even more and the excitement increased.

As I watched from the deck, that crowd mirrored for me all the emotions of mankind, but my introspection and sadness were all swept away by enthusiastic farewell. Passenger ships were not yet back on routine service and I was amongst the fortunate ones to secure early passage on a troop-ship. I felt like an Ambassador from a proud country in the tropics and no doubt other students felt the same.

The clamour grew and the ship's siren had compelling urgency. Everywhere there was movement. Unbelievably rapidly the ship weighed anchor, turned and headed for the open sea. The crowd below faded and blurred and the colours dimmed and the waving handkerchiefs were like a sea of white-wash. With great sadness and yet great hope we were leaving Trinidad.

Countless years on, when I recall that vibrant crowd on the dockside my heart breaks.

271

37

Voyage to the UK via Mexico, Portugal, Spain

Smoothly and swiftly the razor-edged bow of the ship parted the deeper waters of the Caribbean Sea on its way to the Gulf of Mexico. Standing still and looking in the direction from whence we came, transfixed, tearful, I saw what seemed to be a silhouette of the city of Port of Spain rise up on the horizon for a fleeting moment and completely disappear. I was totally baffled by the incident and felt somewhat apprehensive about my venture. However, I soon brushed aside all thoughts and feelings of self-pity, and decided to acquaint myself with new surroundings.

I began with the sleeping quarters. This compartment seemed to be deep down in the bosom of the ship. I never knew the official name of that place but to me it was the bunk room; I was assigned to the fourth tier of a particular row. As such I thought it would be very useful to be able to locate it in the dark should there be electricity failure at any time. If I were to compare the ship with some of the buildings with whose construction I was familiar, I would say that the bunk room was in the very basement. Now, that left me to wondering what was the level of the waterline of the ship when laden, and also when empty, in respect of the floor level of the bunk room. I did not bother to find out. Besides, I realised that it would soon be meal time. I was somewhat hungry to boot.

Now it was mealtime. The signal was given, we entered the dining hall and took our seats at the table. Thick, heavy, matt-finished metal plates and thick heavy knives to match. They all issued a muffled dull thud when placed upon the thick, steel table-top. A thick overweight matching mug, steel or wrought-iron, completed the accoutrements. It all left me totally convinced that I was on a ship specially geared for war, and to all accounts with implements for the use of men trained for war.

Just having cleansed my mind of all dubious thoughts and controversial matters, someone called out, 'Hello, what are you doing there? Meditating I suppose!'

I glanced round and saw the pleasing face I'd seen a little while ago in the dining-hall.

'Hello,' I responded. 'That's amazing, I was just thinking about you; we sat facing each other a short distance away at mealtime I believe.'

'Yes, of course. I am Harry, what's your name?'

'Jacob,' I replied, then added that it has nothing to do with Isaac and Rebecca.

He appreciated the remark and smiled. We both smiled.

'By the way, from your conversation with someone in the dining-hall earlier on, you appeared to have a good idea of what's going on . . . our ports of call and so on,' I explained.

'Well, although I am an ex-serviceman myself, to tell you the truth, I don't know much; the atmosphere is still a bit hush-hush.'

At that moment Harry lowered his voice, and strangely enough I followed suit.

'But why is that necessary?' I asked, perhaps to justify my apprehension when I first entered the ship, I thought to myself.

'You see, there are some German ex-prisoners on this

ship,' Harry continued, 'and to all accounts we may be picking up some more in Mexico, Portugal and Spain before we arrive in Southampton. So there we are,' Harry concluded.

It was rather strange that no sooner I'd got rid of a set of menacing thoughts that another should take its place. This time the disastrous business of lurking German spies programmed for spiteful delayed action, and primed saboteurs with limpet mines at the ready for instantaneous catastrophe. Those thoughts lingered on for a while. With dusk approaching. I decided on an early night to enjoy Mexico the following day. I had learnt Spanish to a much higher degree than necessary for the London Matriculation Examination. I therefore looked forward to some practical usage.

In a glorious blaze of morning sunshine the ship sailed into the Gulf of Mexico and berthed at Veracruz Harbour in the warmth of smiling faces and applause. In due course, a party from our ship was allowed ashore but was not permitted to stay overnight. Furthermore, a deadline was imposed for our return to the ship each night during the period that we were there.

On shore we soon found ourselves split up into small groups and pursued our individual interests. I quietly wandered off by myself, observing the architecture of what appeared to be public buildings. The various types of dwelling houses, roofing, slope and construction materials were foremost in my mind.

During my casual and peaceful observation, I instinctively followed a quiet, narrow, winding street; within minutes, to my surprise and delight, I heard soft melodious voices singing to the sound of enchanting music. I hurried along and just around the corner in the form of a lay-by, sheltered from the glare of the sun, were three men with guitars and maracas. Wearing their wide-brimmed hats and colourful fancy garments, they sang with such deep emotion that stilled the atmosphere. Among their admirers were men, women and children. During a brief interval the leader of the group beckoned me over to a friendly welcome and introduction. I praised their performance and informed them of my journey to Britain. Moreover, I told them that I would be leaving their beautiful country the following day.

They were pleasantly surprised to meet me and on my departure, asked me to return anytime. Being my last day, I made it a point to speak to some of the children. They were apprehensive at first, but in a short while their faces lit up with the pleasure they found in trying to help me speak their language.

Now having decided to return to the ship, I paused on elevated ground overlooking the harbour, and in a manner of reappraisal, silently said, 'That ship brought us all the way from Trinidad, and there she is waiting to take us across the Atlantic Ocean'.

I took a deep breath and went on to board the ship. It was about 5 o'clock in the evening.

The following morning, long before the sun had generated its dazzling brilliance, the ship was on its way out of the Gulf of Mexico and into the Atlantic Ocean. It was not before half an hour had elapsed that the tremendous impact of an overwhelming spectacle began to wear off. Muffled utterances were then heard issuing from the crowd. We had hastened out on deck to get a commanding view of whatever there was to be seen. Well, unexpectedly we were confronted with an awe-inspiring display of exceptional magnitude. It was as though the waters of the mighty ocean and the proverbial firmament had collaborated in sealing their fringes together at the horizon and, in response to their supplication, the sun had cast its hypnotic rays over the entire sea and sky, heralding one of summer's brightest days. It was a moment of Hope and Glory, and it was with that feeling we set off across the Atlantic Ocean for Southampton, calling at Lisbon and Bilbao. Excellent weather prevailed throughout the crossing, and several minor incidents such as the sightings of stray German mines and compulsory fire drills engaged our attention. My chess set was in great demand throughout the journey.

After ten days' voyage in the open sea, we entered Portuguese territorial waters and were soon piloted through the mouth of the River Tagus to dock in Lisbon harbour. It was about 5.30 p.m. and despite the beautiful sunshine, only passengers who were bound for Portugal were permitted to disembark, for an early departure the following morning had been arranged. Everyone seemed to have relished the idea of an early night to bed. A great deal had been said about the notorious waters of the Bay of Biscay and most of us were concerned, or rather curious to know where exactly it was. No doubt retiring early for the night may have been a form of bracing up for the fray.

Early the following morning as expected, there was the usual hustle and bustle at the port in readiness for our ship to be escorted out of the river and away to the open sea. Within minutes of this being done, the ship began a gentle roll as it had done sometime before; and here again it seemed rather pleasant. We were bound for Bilbao and were virtually at the periphery of the notorious waters of the Bay of Biscay. My mind was fully prepared, and made notes of events as best I could. After a little while the gentle roll ceased as though in placid waters. Then changing tactics altogether the ship lunged in a desperate assault upon the onrush of bubbling billows.

At times it was as though the ship had come up against an impregnable wall of water and, realizing the futility of her desperate lunging assaults, had paused to take stock of her armoury. The power of her magnificent engines was unimpaired, and so was the cutting edge of her robust bow. Resolved to continue battle, the ship resorted to a change of tactics yet again. The wall of water was linked to a dense sheet of ice, penetrated by a fierce lunge and lacerated by a vicious up-thrust due to the swell of the sea. At the crest of the upsurge there was a vigorous shudder and a pause, immediately followed by another lunge to begin the cycle all over again. But it was not long before this pattern too had changed. In fact, it alternated with an entirely new form. At the summit of the lunge sequence immediately following the pause, the ship reverted to the gentle roll from side to side. After a few minutes there was a reversion to the lunging tactics, shuddering at the crest of the wave as before. Cycles of this pattern alternated with those of the 'roll' sequence until, at length, the rolling action took over with a most unsettling ferocity.

I saw the superstructure of the ship racing towards the surface of the churning water with an astonishing acceleration to one side and then the other with a pause in the middle. Each roll seemed to venture without restraint to the utmost limitation. I had already retreated to the lounge for safety, but it had suddenly become a danger area.

'All passengers . . . down below to your bunks,' was the repeated order by members of the crew as they dashed about, battening down or fastening up the elusive tables and chairs, some of which were already gliding at speed across the floor of the lounge from port to starboard and back again with the roll of the ship. The odd pieces of furniture and rolling bottles on the floor as yet unretrieved crashed against the partition and ricocheted unpredictably, heightening the already charged atmosphere. Seasickness had begun to run riot just before the orders to go down to our bunks were given. Thus many cups and saucers with rejected contents precariously poised on the table soon joined their counterparts on the floor in shambles. Not having had a history of seasickness, I delayed somewhat to give assistance where needed.

There were moments when the situation in the lounge seemed like a display of tightrope walkers in a circus on the one hand, and a group of drunken revellers on the other. It rose to the peak when the order to clear the room was given and one hustled uncontrollably to the bunk room below. I recall the sound of screaming female voices when the first table took flight and crashed against a partition. However, we soon entered calmer waters to dock at Bilbao for a period of three days.

On leaving Bilbao, a feeling of nostalgia crept over me once again. I was reminded of my departure from my homeland. It was twenty-eight days ago; but there was no feeling of sadness for everyone at that Spanish port was bright and cheerful. I was very impressed since there were no black people among the waiting crowd, and their general attitude towards the black people in our group gave no indication of the prejudices experienced in my homeland.

As such I felt a particular endearment for the Spanish people and was very pleased to realize that not all white people held disdainful views of black people. Soon we were in the English Channel heading for Southampton. Momentarily, the troop-ship signalled her approach to the harbour and a train of feverish stirrings ensued.

I had already gathered my belongings and, at a vantage point as usual, I enjoyed the beautiful landscape of the calm, sailing along the Channel, constantly being greeted by the familiar cries of seagulls. It vaguely entered my head that the gulls had followed me all the way from Trinidad. As the ship drew nearer her berth, anxious eyes began peering down, scanning from one end of the quay to the other in search of a loved one. And heavy sighs of relief followed by sporadic bursts of jubilation were the general order of events.

The excitement grew to a great intensity and sustained that level for quite a while, no doubt symbolic of the great relief of having survived a voyage of nearly thirty days, and the reunion of kith and kin. The camaraderie which had developed among fellow students during the long journey on the ship counted for nothing compared with this moment of triumph and jubilation at the port of our destination.

No time was wasted in the process of disembarkation and groups of relatives and well-wishers joined in lavish greetings of welcome, expressive of tenderness and warm affection. The constant use of my chess set by all and sundry during the Atlantic crossing may have made me a subject of endearment then, and no doubt the confines of the ship, bobbing along for days and nights on such a massive expanse of water, may have forced us all into a superficial role of kith and kin. But now reality had taken over. We had set foot ashore. I thanked the Heavens and Earth for having arrived safely in the land of the Mother Country. My luggage consisted of a large trunk, suit cases and parcels which altogether seemed rather a lot for one person; but I was prepared to stay for a relatively long period. Priority was given to the safety of my belongings, thus I immediately gathered them into a pile on the railway platform, beside me. To all accounts, that was the prevailing state of affairs.

Suddenly, the bristling atmosphere was noticeably subdued. Anxiously looking around, I realized that where but a few moments ago there were other students like myself bustling away, now there were none. They had all vanished and must have been on the train I'd seen disappearing round a bend on its way to London. That

279

was the train I should have caught, but somehow my heart was set on a nearby train, not London-bound. I realized then that with the train I'd seen disappearing round the bend went the lofty promises of introduction to some seasoned city folk from London who may have been sympathetic to the cause of a stranger with a chess set.

Now I felt utterly alone in a foreign country, but one nevertheless, I was taught to regard as the Mother Country. I knew that many more difficult tasks lay ahead and that the next stage was about to begin. Pondering my next move, I sat on my trunk with my other possessions heaped up around it on the platform.

It was late afternoon. The sun was bright but offered little warmth. Soon it would be evening, I thought; but the sun was still high up in the sky . . . so unlike the West Indies.

'I was indeed a stranger in the land,' I said to myself.

While pondering the issues, fleeting moments of doubt as to the wisdom of my undertaking registered in my mind, but my resolve grew stronger in the process. All of a sudden, it was evening. Still seated on my trunk, glancing sideways, at the end of the platform in the distance I saw a lone figure dressed in black advancing towards me in the dwindling light. It was a male figure. His approach was steadfast and deliberate. I knew at once the solution to my predicament was imminent and that I would presently be on my way to London, the capital city of the MOTHER COUNTRY.